D0312499

At Issue

| Sexting

Other Books in the At Issue Series:

At Issue

Sexting

Stefan Kiesbye, Book Editor

GREENHAVEN PRESS
A part of Gale, Cengage Learning

GALE
CENGAGE Learning™

Detroit • New York • San Francisco • New Haven, Conn • Waterville, Maine • London

GALE
CENGAGE Learning·

Christine Nasso, *Publisher*
Elizabeth Des Chenes, *Managing Editor*

© 2011 Greenhaven Press, a part of Gale, Cengage Learning.

Gale and Greenhaven Press are registered trademarks used herein under license.

For more information, contact:
Greenhaven Press
27500 Drake Rd.
Farmington Hills, MI 48331-3535
Or you can visit our Internet site at gale.cengage.com

ALL RIGHTS RESERVED.
No part of this work covered by the copyright herein may be reproduced, transmitted, stored, or used in any form or by any means graphic, electronic, or mechanical, including but not limited to photocopying, recording, scanning, digitizing, taping, Web distribution, information networks, or information storage and retrieval systems, except as permitted under Section 107 or 108 of the 1976 United States Copyright Act, without the prior written permission of the publisher.

For product information and technology assistance, contact us at

Gale Customer Support, 1-800-877-4253
For permission to use material from this text or product, submit all requests online at www.cengage.com/permissions.

Further permissions questions can be e-mailed to permissionrequest@cengage.com.

Articles in Greenhaven Press anthologies are often edited for length to meet page requirements. In addition, original titles of these works are changed to clearly present the main thesis and to explicitly indicate the author's opinion. Every effort is made to ensure that Greenhaven Press accurately reflects the original intent of the authors. Every effort has been made to trace the owners of copyrighted material.

Cover image copyright © Images.com/Corbis.

LIBRARY OF CONGRESS CATALOGING-IN-PUBLICATION DATA

Sexting / Stefan Kiesbye, book editor.
    p. cm. -- (At issue)
    Includes bibliographical references and index.
    ISBN 978-0-7377-5161-1 (hardcover) -- ISBN 978-0-7377-5162-8 (pbk.)
    1. Internet and teenagers. 2. Internet--Safety measures. 3. Teenagers--Sexual relations. 4. Electronic mail systems. I. Kiesbye, Stefan. II. Title. III. Series.
    HQ799.2.I5.S49 2011
    004.67'80835--dc22
                                                            2010047506

Printed in the United States of America
3 4 5 6 7 15 14 13 12 11

Contents

Introduction

In September 2006, a concerned, anonymous mother posted a message on the Berkeley Parents Network website:

> My 14 year old son has just recently been visiting what look to be soft porn sites when he thinks I am not paying attention. We have had all the safety on the internet talks, and I have said "no porn" as a rule. Now I am not sure what to do or how to enforce it. I am a single working mom, so he is home on his own a fair amount, and he stays up later than me. I know it is natural for boys this age to be curious (I remember the stories of our generation's boys finding *Playboys* in their fathers' garages), and I also know that as soon as he realizes I am checking his history he will figure out a way to hide it from me. I don't want to take his computer away, as it brings him so much pleasure & company (he is an only child), & he uses it for research. . . .

In the years before and since, many other parents have expressed concern about their teenagers stumbling upon, or actively seeking out, pornographic websites. Even when parents block their children's computers from displaying pornographic material, teenagers can usually find a way to look at Internet porn—on a friend's laptop, or on the parents' own computers. The rise of cell phones with Internet browsing capabilities makes teenagers' access to porn easier and the parents' job of keeping an eye on their children's activities more difficult.

Parents face the difficult dilemma of either invading their children's privacy or potentially letting the viewing of sometimes deeply disturbing pornographic images and films go unnoticed and, as a consequence, undiscussed. With the advent of sexting—which involves a person's transmitting pictures of themselves, scantily clad or in the nude, via cell phone or other media—parents' concerns have broadened beyond pornographic websites. Parents are displeased that their children are not only consuming porn but also producing and transmitting sexually explicit images. Several commentators have theorized a link between the two, asserting that exposure to pornography and other aspects of a highly sexualized popular culture has contributed to the sexting trend.

Many teens—and sympathetic adults—have professed that transmitting such photos is harmless and playful, a way to project a certain image, entice others into a relationship, or experiment with their sexuality. Such explanations do little to calm anxious parents, though, who fear the repercussions of what is viewed by some as an epidemic. The media have reported alarming cases of sexting-related bullying in which suggestive images of teenagers were forwarded well beyond the intended recipients, sparking aggressive bullying and harassment. In isolated, tragic cases, such harassment has led to suicide. Incidents like these—as well as concerns that a teen's explicit photos could end up in the possession of a sexual predator—have parents frightened for the safety of their kids. A sense of panic about sexting has been stoked by sensationalist reports circulated by the very medium that made sexting possible—the Internet—and the potential connection between teenagers' experimentation and commercial porn sites has seized widespread attention.

Many parents, along with school administrators and law enforcement officials, are struggling to find appropriate methods for detecting and disciplining sexting. Yet the rush to make children safe without a careful consideration of the dangers of overly harsh penalties has already caused its share of travesties. Wired.com reported on January 26, 2008, that a Florida middle school on-campus police officer was facing a criminal investigation over his MySpace account.

> Gulf Middle School resource officer John Nohejl didn't have porn on his MySpace profile, and he didn't link to porn. But one of the 170-odd people on his friends list, which seems mostly populated by students at his school, had a link to a

legal adult site. Now the New Port Richey Police Department and the Florida attorney general's elite cyber crimes unit are investigating him for making adult content available to underage children.

In addition, cases have been reported in which teens have been threatened with charges of child pornography possession because they received nude photos of peers on their cell phones. While no parent wants his or her kids visiting porn sites or being exposed to cyber harassment, rash new measures and harsh punishments for teenagers sending each other nude pictures of themselves might backfire and do more harm than good. And while school administrators and police grapple with the viral aspect of new technologies, they might, as the above example shows, put themselves in harm's way.

At Issue: Sexting explores a range of views on the issue, including possible causes for teenagers' actions, parents' and teenagers' fears, the ramifications of new ways of communication open to teens, and the possible need to craft new laws in an age when emerging technologies are changing our culture at an ever-increasing rate.

1

Sexting Puts Teenagers and Young Adults at Risk

Libby Quaid

Libby Quaid is an education writer for the Associated Press, a global news network.

The practice of sending nude pictures by cell phone is widespread and can have serious consequences. What is considered by many high school students as flirtatious and sexy—and by some parents as merely stupid or thoughtless—can have legal ramifications, however, since many states are cracking down on this new phenomenon by charging teenagers with possession of child pornography. Furthermore, many parents and officials are concerned that nude pictures "going viral" can lead to bullying and harassment and, in extreme cases, to victims' suicides.

Think your kid is not "sexting"? Think again.

Sexting—sharing sexually explicit photos, videos and chat by cell phone or online—is fairly commonplace among young people, despite sometimes grim consequences for those who do it. More than a quarter of young people have been involved in sexting in some form, an Associated Press [AP]-MTV poll found.

That includes Sammy, a 16-year-old from the San Francisco Bay Area who asked that his last name not be used.

Libby Quaid, "'Sexting' More Common than You Might Think," *Los Angeles Daily News*, December 3, 2009. Copyright © 2009 by Press Association, Inc. Reproduced by permission.

Sharing Naked Pictures

Sammy said he had shared naked pictures of himself with girlfriends. He also shared naked pictures of someone else that a friend had sent him.

What he didn't realize at the time was that young people across the country—in Florida, Indiana, Ohio and Pennsylvania—have faced charges, in some cases felony charges, for sending nude pictures.

"That's why I probably wouldn't do it again," Sammy said.

Yet, "I just don't see it as that big of a problem, personally."

That was the view of nearly half of those surveyed who have been involved in sexting. The other half said it's a serious problem—and did it anyway. Knowing there might be consequences hasn't stopped them.

Research shows teenage brains are not quite mature enough to make good decisions consistently.

"There's definitely the invincibility factor that young people feel," said Kathleen Bogle, a sociology professor at La Salle University in Philadelphia and author of the book *Hooking Up: Sex, Dating and Relationships on Campus.*

"That's part of the reason why they have a high rate of car accidents and things like that, is they think, 'Oh, well, that will never happen to me,'" Bogle said.

A Matter of Development

Research shows teenage brains are not quite mature enough to make good decisions consistently. By the mid-teens, the brain's reward centers, the parts involved in emotional arousal, are well-developed, making teens more vulnerable to peer pressure.

But it is not until the early 20s that the brain's frontal cortex, where reasoning connects with emotion, enabling people to weigh consequences, has finished forming.

Beyond feeling invincible, young people also have a much different view of sexual photos that might be posted online, Bogle said. They don't think about the idea that those photos might wind up in the hands of potential employers or college admissions officers, she said.

"Sometimes they think of it as a joke; they have a laugh about it," Bogle said. "In some cases, it's seen as flirtation. They're thinking of it as something far less serious and aren't thinking of it as consequences down the road or who can get hold of this information. They're also not thinking about worst-case scenarios that parents might worry about."

Boys were more likely to say that sexting is "hot," while most girls called it "slutty."

Sexting doesn't stop with teenagers. Young adults are even more likely to have sexted; one-third of them said they had been involved in sexting, compared with about one-quarter of teenagers.

Thelma, a 25-year-old from Natchitoches, La., who didn't want her last name used, said she's been asked more than once to send naked pictures of herself to a man.

"It's just when you're talking to a guy who's interested in you, and you might have a sexual relationship, so they just want to see you naked," she said, adding that she never complied with those requests.

"But with my current boyfriend, I did it on my own; he didn't ask me," she said, adding that she was confident he would keep the image to himself.

A Romantic Gesture

Those who sent nude pictures of themselves mostly said they went to a boyfriend, girlfriend or romantic interest.

But 14 percent said they suspect the pictures were shared without permission, and they may be right: Seventeen percent of those who received naked pictures said they passed them along to someone else, often to more than just one person.

Boys were a little more likely than girls to say they received naked pictures or video of someone that had been passed around without the person's consent. Common reasons were that they thought other people would want to see, that they were showing off and that they were bored.

Girls were a little more likely to send pictures of themselves. Yet boys were more likely to say that sexting is "hot," while most girls called it "slutty."

Altogether, 10 percent said they had sent naked pictures of themselves on their cell phone or online.

Criminal charges aren't the worst consequences. In at least two cases, sexting has been linked to suicide. Last year [2008] in Cincinnati, [Ohio,] 18-year-old Jessica Logan hanged herself after weeks of ridicule at school; she had sent a nude cell phone picture to her boyfriend, and after they broke up, he forwarded the picture to other girls.

And three months ago [in September 2009], 13-year-old Hope Witsell hanged herself, after relentless taunting at her school near Tampa, Fla. She had sent a nude photo of herself to a boy she liked, and another girl used his phone to send the picture to other students who forwarded it along. The *St. Petersburg Times* first reported on Hope's death this week [December 2009].

Cyberbullying Is Dangerous

Other teenage suicides have been linked to online bullying, also a subject of the AP-MTV poll. Half of all young people said they have been targets of digital bullying.

That can mean someone wrote something about them on the Internet that was mean or a lie, or someone shared an e-mail or instant message that was supposed to be private.

Less often, it can be more serious, such as taking pictures or video of someone in a sexual situation and sharing it with others.

The AP-MTV poll was conducted Sept. 11–22, [2009,] and involved online interviews with 1,247 teenagers and adults ages 14–24. It has a margin of sampling error of plus or minus 2.8 percentage points.

The poll is part of an MTV campaign, "A Thin Line," aiming to stop the spread of digital abuse.

2

The Threat of Sexting Has Been Exaggerated

Daniel Greene

Daniel Greene is an American Sign Language interpreter, singer, actor, and dancer. He has been writing for his website, daniel greene.com, since 1996.

Sexting is only a way for teenagers to express themselves in the context of a new technology. Parents and lawmakers, however, try to shame them with unsubstantiated arguments that sexting leads to an increase in teen pregnancy and bullying as well as violations of privacy. Instead of prosecuting teens as child pornographers, parents should teach their children that representations of the naked body do not diminish self-worth.

Listening to NPR's [National Public Radio's] *All Things Considered* just now [in March 2009], I heard a story on sexting—teens sending photos of each other naked via text messages—that got me to thinking "what exactly is the big deal?" I don't ask that question to minimize the phenomenon, but to analyze it for the social taboos that are being broken here.

The Problem of Shame

I recently finished reading *The Cluetrain Manifesto*, and its message about people finding their voice on the Internet and how this might change issues of privacy had me listening in a

Daniel Greene, "Sexting Highlights Society's Issues with Privacy and Shame," Daniel Greene.com, March 11, 2009. Copyright © Daniel Greene. Reprinted by permission of the author and literary agent Jill Marr.

certain way. One of my favorite questions one of the authors of *Cluetrain* asks is, "What would privacy be like if it weren't connected to shame?"

Indeed, none of this "sexting" would be an issue if it weren't for shame—shame that teens may or may not feel about their developing bodies, shame that adults may or may not feel looking at photos of teen bodies, and all the nebulous shame that society places upon the naked human body.

What's the big deal if kids want to show each other their naked bodies?

What if these kids aren't ashamed of their bodies? What if, as the authors of *Cluetrain* assert, people gravitate toward the Internet to satisfy the age-old human desire for self-expression? Maybe these kids are just using these media to express themselves, to say, "Look at me. I exist. I'm unique. Yet I'm a lot like you." Aren't adults heaping shame upon these kids by charging them with felony child pornography? What's the big deal if kids want to show each other their naked bodies? "It may lead to teen pregnancy!" Yes, it may. So may having sex without a condom and/or birth control medication. But I seriously doubt that "sexting" is bringing about a rise in teen pregnancy.

The Issue of Privacy

So, what is the issue? Well, privacy is a big part of it, and it goes along with distribution. To whom are they distributing the nude photographs? Maybe to a few friends, maybe just to one. But if that one friend distributes it to others until it becomes distributed exponentially like viral Internet media, whom do we blame for the distribution? Do we blame the first sender who "should have known better" than to send *anyone* a nude photograph of themselves knowing that it might end up in the wrong hands? Or do we blame the subsequent distributors? What if the exact chain of distribution could be traced? Do we blame each and every one? Where does this distribution cross the line from acceptable to unacceptable? When does the private become public?

I faced some of these questions when I took an artistic nude photograph of myself that I wanted to share. Why did I want to share it? Well, because I liked the way I looked and I liked the way I took the photo. Was my intent to titillate? No. Was it pornography? Well, not to me. My penis wasn't even visible, for whatever that's worth. I questioned myself when I published the photo to my Flickr account. Should I mark it Public or Private? Should I mark it Private: Friends Only or Private: Friends & Family Only? If I marked it for Family & Friends Only, would my family and friends feel I singled them out for the viewing of this nude photo? I didn't want that. So I used Flickr's SafeSearch filters to flag the photo "Moderate" ("may be considered offensive by some people"). That way, only those people who have their SafeSearch browsing settings on "Moderate" ("You're OK seeing the odd 'artistic nude' here or there, but that's the limit") will see the photo, be they friends or strangers.

I think as long as no one is forcing these kids to be photographed naked, it's not pornography.

Filtering Content Appropriately

Socially, it seems acceptable to display yourself nude in an artistic venue as long as you're not personally flashing people. And I'm all about filtering my content so that people see only what they're comfortable with seeing (when it comes to nudity, that is). Yet, I am not so naïve as to think that just because I published a photo on Flickr with SafeSearch filters means that no one else will ever see it. I know that a photo on Flickr can be taken out of Flickr, indeed, taken out of context. I have to laugh at what Brian Shaler [a web developer] said in his Twitter bio: "Take me out of context." (He's since changed his bio, but that's what it said last time I looked.) So, yes, people may take me out of context. But I am okay with that because, as one young nude man so eloquently said in an avant-garde play I once saw, "I am irreducible. My nakedness does not diminish me."

What if we lived in a world in which a person's nakedness did not diminish them? What if it didn't matter if teenage girls took photos of themselves in the shower and the whole world saw it? I know we don't live in that world, but I can imagine it. I think as long as no one is forcing these kids to be photographed naked, it's not pornography. So what if these kids are playing Doctor on their cell phones? Maybe we should spend less of our energy trying to control *their* use of *our* technology and more energy on fostering an "irreducible" self-esteem in children of all ages.

3

Sexting-Related Bullying Can Have Dire Consequences

Andrew Meacham

Andrew Meacham is a reporter for the St. Petersburg (FL) Times *and writes for the* South Shore & Brandon Times *on a wide variety of human interest topics and breaking news.*

Hope Witsell, a teenager and middle school student, killed herself after an image of her topless, sent to one boy only, was forwarded to many others, exposing her to nasty bullying and harassment in school. What started as a flirtatious gesture soon became the source of anguish for the student, because the photo, and other students' perceptions of Hope, refused to go away. In a society fraught with sexual imagery and innuendo, it is important to teach young people that sexting has the power to breach their privacy and haunt them forever.

A t the end of the school year at Beth Shields Middle School [in Ruskin, Florida], the taunting became so bad that Hope Witsell's friends surrounded her between classes. They escorted her down hallways like human shields, fending off insults such as "whore" and "slut." A few days before, Hope had forwarded a nude photo of herself to a boy she liked—a practice widely known as "sexting." The image found its way to other students, who forwarded it to their friends. Soon the nude photo was circulating through cell phones at Shields Middle and [nearby] Lennard High School, according to mul-

Andrew Meacham, "Sexting-Related Bullying Cited in Hillsborough Teen's Suicide," *St. Petersburg Times*, November 29, 2009. Copyright © 2009 by St. Petersburg Times. Reproduced by permission.

tiple students at both schools. "Tons of people talk about me behind my back and I hate it because they call me a whore!" Hope wrote in her journal. "And I can't be a whore I'm too inexperienced. So secretly TONS of people hate me ..." School authorities learned of the nude photo around the end of the school year and suspended Hope for the first week of eighth grade, which started in August [2009]. About two weeks after she returned to school, a counselor observed cuts on Hope's legs and had her sign a "no-harm" contract, in which Hope agreed to tell an adult if she felt inclined to hurt herself, her family says. The next day, Hope hanged herself in her bedroom. She was 13.

A 2009 Harris online poll shows that one in five teens admits to having sent naked pictures of themselves or others over a cell phone.

The Link Between Suicide and Sexting

Her death is the second in the nation in which a connection between sexting and teen suicide can clearly be drawn.

"This is very important, because it shows that sexting-related suicides are tracking the same way cyberbullying-related suicides are," said Parry Aftab, a nationally known "cyberlawyer" who has appeared on *Good Morning America* and the *Today* show.

A 2009 Harris online poll shows that one in five teens admits to having sent naked pictures of themselves or others over a cell phone. But even that number may be low.

Hope grew up in Sundance, an isolated rural suburb 6 miles off U.S. 41 in south Hillsborough County. Her parents, Donna and Charlie Witsell, met in the post office where they both work. They married in 1995. Hope was their only child together. They took her to church every Sunday.

Hope wasn't a troubled girl. She was an "A" and "B" student in all subjects but math. She had many friends, whom she liked to give bear hugs. She often went fishing with her father in her big, white-framed sunglasses. On mornings when she was running late to school, Hope carried her cereal and milk in a coffee cup and ate on the bus.

Hope knew exactly what she wanted to do with her life: attend the University of Florida and major in agriculture. Then she would start a landscaping and nursery business.

Like many other girls her age, she was boy-crazy.

Tacked to her bedroom door beneath a *Twilight* poster of the vampire Edward Cullen is a piece of notebook paper folded in quarters. It is a note from a boy, one line written in faint pencil:

"U still like me?"

A Moment of Poor Judgment

Accounts vary, but many students describe the chain of events this way: The last week of school in June, Hope forwarded a photo of her breasts to the cell phone of Alex Eargood, a boy she liked. A rival girl, who was the girlfriend of another boy Hope liked and a friend of Alex's, asked to borrow Alex's phone on the bus. That girl found the image and forwarded it to other students.

Alex, now 16 and a freshman at Armwood High School, told the *St. Petersburg Times* last week [in November 2009] that he deleted the photo. He does not remember whether he deleted it before or after the girl borrowed his phone. The mother of the girl told the *Times* that her daughter would not comment for this article.

Within hours, the image had gone viral at Shields and Lennard High.

"People were getting it at school and sending it at school," said Lane James, 14, a friend of Hope's at Shields Middle. "The hallways were not fun at that time."

Lane, who shared four classes with Hope last year, called the atmosphere around school that week "brutal."

"She'd walk into class and somebody would say, 'Oh, here comes the slut,'" Lane said.

At the same time, friends say, Hope knew that the biggest mistakes made were her own.

"She didn't blame it on anybody," said Rebecca Knowles, 14. "She realized it was her fault for sending them in the first place."

The speed of the Internet and the ubiquity of social networking sites like MySpace and Facebook make it that much harder to escape the embarrassment.

The Sexting Epidemic

Sexting, defined as the sharing of nude or seminude images over a cell phone or a computer, is growing among teenagers, including young teens. The Harris poll showed that 9 percent of 13-year-olds admitted doing it—even though most teens polled believe it is wrong to send nude photos of minors to others.

Aftab, who in April led a town meeting on teen sexting with *Good Morning America's* Diane Sawyer, noted that teens who participated in the Harris poll needed their parents' consent. She believes the real number of teen sexters to be much higher.

A poll conducted by her organization, WiredSafety, found that 44 percent of boys in co-ed high schools had seen at least one naked picture of a female classmate. Overwhelmingly, they shared the images with others.

Early adolescents like Hope face the biggest psychological risks, Aftab said. An 11-year-old doesn't have as many hormones, while a 16-year old may have developed enough of a social network to cushion the blow.

"The real risk is the 12- and 13-year age," she said.

The speed of the Internet and the ubiquity of social networking sites like MySpace and Facebook make it that much harder to escape the embarrassment. It also means the photos may never go away.

Dire Consequences

"If they are sexting images that are being made public, they are going to be tagged forever as a slut," Aftab said. "So they don't see a future. And if they don't see a future, they (think they) might as well end their life. We are seeing a lot of that in this age."

The social consequences can be even worse for high-performing teens who consider themselves "good kids," said Yale psychiatrist Robert King.

"There are some kids who are very self-critical and very demanding of themselves, and see any kind of setback or embarrassment as just a humiliating catastrophe," said King, a professor of child psychiatry at the Yale Child Study Center and an expert on teenage suicide. "It sort of sounds like that's the flavor of kid she was."

Those types of kids also are more likely to keep their deepest emotions hidden from their parents, experts say. That was the case with Hope. When she was feeling down, she wrote about it in her journal but did not confide in her parents.

"Hope certainly did not let on that something was wrong," said Charlie Witsell, 46. "She never really said anything to us."

Two weeks after school let out, the school learned of the nude photo and called Charlie and Donna Witsell for a conference. Officials issued the one-week suspension for the fall.

The Witsells confiscated Hope's cell phone and computer and grounded her for the summer. They were dismayed, but also thought it could be a learning opportunity.

"In a strange way I was glad she got caught, because at least that way we got to see what's going on," Charlie Witsell said.

Hope said she was sorry for her actions, which she could not explain. She vowed to undergo her punishment and start the new school year afresh.

Hope would, however, be allowed to attend the annual FFA [Future Farmers of America] convention in Orlando, less than two weeks after the end of the school year. The convention rewards students for their work in statewide agriculture competitions.

Peer Pressure and Bullying

An FFA student adviser for her school before the incident, Hope was due to pick up at least two awards: a first-place team award for nursery and landscaping, plus her individual trophy for the highest test score in the state for her age group in that category.

No one knows how Hope met a group of boys staying across the hall. Rebecca Knowles, who is the FFA president, saw Hope talking to the boys by the hotel pool.

The boys were in their late teens and were not there for the FFA convention. They insisted she send a nude photo to them.

One of the boys was especially aggressive and called the room repeatedly on the conference's last night, asking Hope for a photo of her breasts.

"They kept calling and they kept bugging her," said Rebecca, 14, who said she was in the room but asleep. "I think she was just scared. One of our roommates was scared as well and said, 'Oh, my God, just do it.' They were scared and wanted to get it over."

The boy calling didn't have a cell phone. So Hope used Rebecca's phone to take a picture of her breasts, then slipped it outside her door.

The phone, which Hope had left outside for the boy, was still in the hallway when an adult found it and saw the photo.

After the incident in Orlando, Charlie and Donna Witsell decided to take Hope to a Christian counselor. After the third visit, the counselor told Donna that Hope didn't want to be there. Forcing her to come wouldn't do any good, the counselor said. Reluctantly, Hope's parents agreed.

Just the same, the quiet, introspective summer seemed to be doing Hope some good. The parents made a few exceptions to her grounding—a sleepover with a friend, a family vacation in Sanibel.

Hope fretted that there would be further consequences over her actions in the spring. She especially worried that she might lose a chance to run again for FFA student adviser.

Hope's parents say no one from the school called them to say their daughter might harm herself.

Ongoing Repercussions

"Making mistakes &/or stupid choices doesn't necessarily make it impossible for you to give advice and lead people in the right direction," she wrote in her journal. "Do you think people ever told Elvis Presley he couldn't lead people to be singers & give them advice because he had made some bad choices with drugs & alcohol? . . . I don't think so!"

While serving her suspension week at the end of August, Hope and her mother stopped by Shields for a status update. There her mother learned that the school would not allow Hope to run for student adviser that year.

Lane James, who was in the office at the time, remembers seeing Hope after that meeting.

"She was in the corner, just bawling and bawling," Lane said. "She wouldn't talk to anybody."

About a week after Hope's suspension ended, she and Rebecca found three boys seated at the cafeteria table the girls had always claimed as their own.

The ringleader, Rebecca said, hectored Hope about the photo that had made its way through the school in June. Another boy joined in.

Hope left the table in tears. She spent the rest of the day in the office talking to counselors, her mother said.

Hope stayed home from school the next day. While her parents were at work, she cleaned the house top to bottom.

What happened at school on Friday, Sept. 11, remains an open question. Samantha Beattie, Hope's aunt, gives the following version of events she said Hope gave to her.

Hope met that day with Jodi Orlando, the school's social worker. Another staff member had noticed cuts on Hope's leg and become concerned.

The social worker quizzed Hope, then had her sign a "no-harm" contract in which Hope agreed to talk to an adult if she felt an urge to hurt herself. Both Orlando and Hope signed the undated contract, which her parents found in Hope's bedroom trash can after her death.

Hope's parents say no one from the school called them to say their daughter might harm herself.

The Hillsborough County School District, through spokeswoman Linda Cobbe, declined to comment on Hope Witsell's interaction with school officials or her suicide, saying officials were prohibited by law from discussing student discipline matters.

Harassment Led to Suicide

Donna and Charlie Witsell both worked Saturday, Sept. 12, Hope stayed home and cut the grass.

On his way home, Charlie stopped by the grocery store for shrimp and crab legs. The family ate seafood that night.

At 8:30 p.m., the phone rang. Hope sprang to answer it. When her parents asked who it was, she answered, "Theresa."

The caller ID, which appeared on the television screen, said "Michael," the name of a 15-year-old boy Hope liked.

Donna heard a boy's voice on the extension. Because she had lied, Hope's parents grounded her from the phone for a week.

At 9:10 p.m., Donna checked on Hope in her room to see if she was all right. She found the girl lying on her bed, writing in her journal. Hope said she was fine.

But Hope was not okay. She wrote in her journal:

Sept. 12, 2009

I'm done for sure now. I can feel it in my stomach. I'm going to try and strangle myself. I hope it works.

We want to think our child is going to learn and grow and develop the skills to make the right choices. They don't have a chance in hell.

A few minutes after 10 p.m., Donna checked in again to see if Hope wanted to come downstairs and watch television with them. Hope declined.

About an hour later, Donna eased open Hope's door again to kiss her good night. She saw her daughter standing a few feet away—her head lowered, her hair was hanging over her face.

"Hope, what are you doing?" Donna said.

Then she saw that a pink scarf was knotted around the canopy of her queen-sized bed. The other end was wrapped around Hope's neck.

Downstairs, Charlie was about to let the dog out when he heard Donna's voice.

"Call 911!"

An ambulance arrived and took Hope to a local hospital, where she was pronounced dead.

The Hillsborough County Medical Examiner's Office ruled Hope's death a suicide. The doctor who examined her body found a "zone of shallow cuts" up to an inch or so long on her right thigh.

A Lack of Communication

One Hillsborough School District official agreed to speak generally about how schools handle students who may be suicide risks. And that would involve a call to the parents if the threat of suicide seemed real.

"If it's felt that students are at risk for harming themselves, there is a followup with parents," said Tracy Schatzberg, the psychological services supervisor for Hillsborough schools. "We would involve parents depending on the level of risk."

Said Donna Witsell: "They dropped the ball big time."

As for sexting, the school district said it routinely presents information to all students about the perils of the practice.

The Hillsborough County Sheriff's Office has finished its investigation into Hope's death, but a sheriff's spokesman said they are still at work on another aspect of the case.

"The whole issue of the nude photograph being distributed through cell phones, we're still looking at," said spokesman J.D. Callaway.

Florida law considers the possession or distribution of nude images of minors to be child pornography, a third-degree felony punishable by up to five years in prison.

Hope's case is the second known sexting-related suicide in the country. The first received national attention.

Jessie Logan was an attractive high school senior in the Cincinnati area who forwarded nude images of herself to a boyfriend at his request.

After they broke up, the boyfriend forwarded the photos to others. The images spread through her high school. Logan,

18, tried to tackle the issue head-on, going on a television news program and urging other teens not to repeat her mistake.

She found it harder to endure the humiliation of walking the halls at school, where other students called her a "porn queen," dumped drinks on her and threw her out of graduation parties.

Two months later, her mother found her hanging in her bedroom.

Growing Up in a Hypersexual Culture

After Hope's death, Charlie and Donna Witsell retraced their steps many times, looking for clues they might have missed.

"Should I have been more careful about what I allowed her to watch?" Donna, 48, said. "Should I have been more careful about what I allowed her to read? Should I have been more careful about restricting her relationships with the opposite sex? There's a fine, fine line, especially when our kids become adolescents. They are maturing way sooner than they used to."

Whenever the Witsells asked Hope how she was feeling after the sexting incident, she always said she was fine. It was only after her death that they found the no-harm contract, deeply despairing diary entries and complex pencil doodlings drawn in class that referred to death and suicide.

The Witsells are coming forward because they feel Hope's sexting incident is a just a symptom of a larger problem: the hyper-sexualization in media aimed at young teens, which they believe forces young minds to contend with ideas of lust and love that they have trouble understanding.

They hope other teens and parents can learn from Hope and avoid the same tragic end.

"Have you been reading these teen magazines lately?" Donna asked. "'How many ways can you turn your boyfriend on? How sexy can you kiss?' We want to think our child is going to learn and grow and develop the skills to make the right choices. They don't have a chance in hell. These kids are bombarded."

4

Sexting-Related Bullying Can Drive Teenagers to Despair

Mike Celizic

Among sportswriter Mike Celizic's published books is The Biggest Game of Them All: Notre Dame, Michigan State and the Fall of 1966. *Celizic is a writer, an adjunct professor of English, and a magazine and newspaper editor.*

After breaking up with her boyfriend, Jesse Logan had to watch helplessly as the nude pictures she sent him were sent to other girls in her school. School officials seem to have been slow to respond to the ensuing bullying and were unable to stop it. Hoping to prevent others from making the same mistake, Jesse went public with her case. In the end, however, the harassment proved too much, and she committed suicide. While many of the teenagers who are sending or receiving nude pictures are minors, older students might be prosecuted as sex offenders as part of an effort to suppress harmful cyberbullying. Parents should be aware of the dangers of sexting and teach their children responsible use of new technologies.

The image was blurred and the voice distorted, but the words spoken by a young Ohio woman are haunting. She had sent nude pictures of herself to a boyfriend. When they broke up, he sent them to other high school girls. The girls were harassing her, calling her a slut and a whore. She was miserable and depressed, afraid even to go to school.

Mike Celizic, "Her Teen Committed Suicide over 'Sexting,'" MSNBC.com, March 6, 2009. Copyright © 2009 by MSNBC.com. Reproduced by permission.

And now Jesse Logan was going on a Cincinnati television station to tell her story. Her purpose was simple: "I just want to make sure no one else will have to go through this again."

The interview was in May 2008. Two months later, Jessica Logan hanged herself in her bedroom. She was 18.

Conveying the Message

"She was vivacious. She was fun. She was artistic. She was compassionate. She was a good kid," the young woman's mother, Cynthia Logan, told *TODAY*'s Matt Lauer [in March 2009] in New York. Still grieving over the loss of her daughter, she said she is taking her story public to warn kids about the dangers of sending sexually charged pictures and messages to boyfriends and girlfriends.

"It's very, very difficult. She's my only child," Logan told Lauer. "I'm trying my best to get the message out there."

It is a growing problem that has resulted in child pornography charges being filed against some teens across the nation. But for Cynthia Logan, "sexting" is about more than possibly criminal activity: It's about life and death.

When she would come to school, she would always hear, "Oh, that's the girl who sent the picture. She's just a whore."

Last fall, the National Campaign to Prevent Teen and Unplanned Pregnancy surveyed teens and young adults about sexting—sending sexually charged material via cell phone text messages—or posting such materials online. The results revealed that 39 percent of teens are sending or posting sexually suggestive messages, and 48 percent reported receiving such messages.

The Devastating Effects of Bullying

Jesse Logan's mother said she never knew the full extent of her daughter's anguish until it was too late. Cynthia Logan only learned there was a problem at all when she started getting daily letters from her daughter's school reporting that the young woman was skipping school.

"I only had snapshots, bits and pieces, until the very last semester of school," Logan told Lauer.

She took away her daughter's car and drove her to school herself, but Jesse still skipped classes. She told her mother there were pictures involved and that a group of younger girls who had received them were harassing her, calling her vicious names, even throwing objects at her. But she didn't realize the full extent of her daughter's despair.

"She was being attacked and tortured," Logan said.

"When she would come to school, she would always hear, 'Oh, that's the girl who sent the picture. She's just a whore,'" Jesse's friend, Lauren Taylor, told NBC News.

Logan said that officials at Sycamore High School were aware of the harassment but did not take sufficient action to stop it. She said that a school official offered only to go to one of the girls who had the pictures and tell her to delete them from her phone and never speak to Jesse again. That girl was 16.

Logan suggested talking to the parents of the girls who were bullying Jesse, but her daughter said that would only open her to even more ridicule.

"She said, 'No, I need to do something else. I'm going to go on the news,' and that's what she did," Logan said.

Finding Jesse

When Cynthia Logan decided to go public with her story, she told Lauer that a school official told a local television station that he had given Jesse the option of prosecuting her tormentors. "That was not so. It's absolutely not true," she told Lauer. "And if he did, why didn't I get a notice in the mail that he gave her that option?"

After her daughter's death, Logan quit her job and was hospitalized for a time with what she described as a mental breakdown. When she spoke about finding her daughter in her bedroom last July, tears coursed down her cheeks.

Jesse had been talking about going to the University of Cincinnati to study graphic design. Her mother thought she was over the worst of the bullying. Then one of Jesse's acquaintances committed suicide. Jesse went to the funeral. When she came home, she hanged herself.

"I just had a scan of the room, her closet doors were open," Logan told NBC News. "And I walked over into her room and saw her hanging. The cell phone was in the middle of the floor."

Quest for Justice

Logan said she's been through six lawyers in what has so far been an unsuccessful battle to hold school officials responsible for the bullying of her daughter.

She was joined on *TODAY* by Parry Aftab, an Internet security expert and activist in the battle to protect teens from the dangers that lurk in cyberspace. Aftab said that there are laws that apply.

"There absolutely is a law," Aftab told Lauer. "It depends on the age of the child. If somebody's under the age of 18, it's child pornography, and even the girl that posted the pictures can be charged. They could be registered sex offenders at the end of all of this. Even at the age of 18, because it was sent to somebody under age, it's disseminating pornography to a minor. There are criminal charges that could be made here."

Aftab said that it is normal kids just like Jesse who fall victim to the perils of the Internet and the easy exchange of information on cell phones.

"We talked about her being a good kid, a normal kid. Those are most of the ones that are sending out those images," she said. "Forty-four percent of the boys say that they've seen sexual images of girls in their school, and about 15 percent of them are disseminating those images when they break up with the girls."

Aftab asked Logan to join her in her fight against the electronic exploitation of kids. "I'm going to get her involved in a huge campaign to allow kids to understand the consequences of this and allow schools to understand what they need to do to keep our kids alive," she said.

Aftab turned to Logan to see if she would help.

"Absolutely," she said.

5

Sexting Should Be Illegal

Dave Yost

Dave Yost is a prosecuting attorney and a former auditor in Delaware County, Ohio.

Sexting is a serious problem, but attempts thus far to rein in teenagers' behavior have been misguided, because they either threaten minors with charges of child pornography or deny the dangers sexual predators pose online. For the fight against sexting to have any success, new legislation is needed to curb new technologies. These laws should make sexting a specific criminal offense but should not brand young people convicted of the offense as sex offenders.

"Sexting"—the practice of girls sending nude photographs of themselves to others via cell phone—is highly dangerous, but not in ways we might at first think. We rarely need to add new laws to the embarrassing tangle that is our criminal code, but in this case, we do. Let's think it through.

A Fruitless and Misguided Debate

The debate about sexting has focused along the tired lines of teen sexuality, and children's freedom to behave badly. A number of my law-and-order colleagues have pointed out that these photographs may be used in embarrassing ways, especially if that middle-school or high-school relationship turns out not to last forever. In Cincinnati, [Ohio,] Jessica Logan

Dave Yost, "Why 'Sexting' Should Be Illegal," DaveYost.com, April 9, 2009. Copyright © 2009 by DaveYost.com. Reproduced by permission.

hanged herself last summer [2008] after her boyfriend shared her sexted photos and they were widely disseminated.

On the other side, predictably, is the American Civil Liberties Union [ACLU].

"What we don't need to do is prosecute children for making mistakes. Children do foolish things and the remedy against foolish things is not criminal action," ACLU lawyer Jeffrey Gamso told the Cincinnati *Enquirer*. "Local officials are twisting the law to prosecute those they were meant to protect. A conviction for sexting can do far more than teach a lesson—it can ruin a life."

Well. Criminal activity always involves "foolish things," Mr Gamso. If foolishness were a defense, prisons would be empty.

Children who "sext" ought not be treated as child pornographers.

New Legislation Necessary

Both sides are missing the point. The problem is with the technology. Digital photographs can be reproduced at zero cost, and sent anywhere in the world. And that world has a sickening number of grown men who stoke their lusts with photographs of naked underage girls.

The first time that image leaves the boyfriend's phone, it is in play. If sexting is treated as a casual and harmless rite of passage, our society will open the door to a huge new source of child pornography, and it will become impossible to police.

Children who "sext" ought not be treated as child pornographers. In particular, it makes zero sense to require a child to become a juvenile registered sex offender. But we need to recognize that this isn't a matter between two middle school or high school sweethearts, but a matter of public policy to prevent the creation of the kind of images sexual predators crave.

That will require a new law, with serious consequences, and prosecution to match. State Representative Ron Maag,

R-Lebanon [Ohio], will soon introduce a specific sexting law that will create a specific criminal offense, with no registration requirements. He's on the right track.

6

The Problem of Sexting Cannot Be Solved by Police and Lawmakers

Judith Levine

Author and journalist Judith Levine's best-known book, Harmful to Minors: The Perils of Protecting Children from Sex, *won the 2002* Los Angeles Times Book Prize. *Her articles have appeared in many national magazines, and she speaks widely at schools and conferences and in the media.*

Sexting and cyberbullying, at their cores, are nothing new. Teenagers behave the way they always did, only with new technologies. And while bullying can be a dangerous consequence of sexting, police and legislators should not criminalize the exchange of nude pictures and stamp minors as sex offenders. Inappropriately severe punishment can only harm teenagers. Instead, adults should be aware of the fact that what may appear to them as disturbingly explicit images is harmless play for their children.

A couple of weeks ago [January 2009], in Greensburg, Pennsylvania, prosecutors charged six teenagers with creating, distributing, and possessing child pornography. The three girls, ages 14 and 15, took nude or seminude pictures of themselves and e-mailed them to friends, including three boys, ages 16 and 17, who are among the defendants. Police Captain George Seranko described the obscenity of the images: They "weren't just breasts," he declared. "They showed female anatomy!"

Judith Levine, "What's the Matter with Teen-Sexting?" *The American Prospect*, February 2, 2009. Copyright © 2009 by The American Prospect. Reproduced by permission.

Greensburg's crime-stoppers aren't the only ones looking out for the cybersafety of America's youth. In Alabama, Connecticut, Florida, New Jersey, New York, Michigan, Ohio, Pennsylvania, Texas, and Utah (at last count) minors have been arrested for "sexting," or sending or posting soft-core photo or video self-portraits. Of 1,280 teens and young adults surveyed recently by the National Campaign to Prevent Teen and Unplanned Pregnancy, one in five said they engaged in the practice—girls only slightly more than boys.

Seranko and other authorities argue that such pictures may find their way to the Internet and from there to pedophiles and other exploiters. "It's very dangerous," he opined.

Sex and predatory adults are not the biggest dangers kids face as they travel the Net.

How dangerous is it? Not very, suggests a major study released this month [February 2009] by Harvard's Berkman Center for Internet Studies. "Enhancing Child Safety and Online Technologies," the result of a yearlong investigation by a wide range of experts, concludes that "the risks minors face online are in most cases not significantly different from those they face offline, and as they get older, minors themselves contribute to some of the problems." Almost all youth who end up having sex with adults they meet online seek such assignations themselves, fully aware that the partner is older. Similarly, minors who encounter pornography online go looking for it; they tend to be older teenage boys.

But sex and predatory adults are not the biggest dangers kids face as they travel the Net. Garden-variety kid-on-kid meanness, enhanced by technology, is. "Bullying and harassment, most often by peers, are the most frequent threats that minors face, both online and offline," the report found.

Just as almost all physical and sexual abuse is perpetrated by someone a child knows intimately—the adult who eats dinner or goes to church with her—victims of cyber-bullying usually know their tormenters: other students who might sit beside them in homeroom or chemistry. Social-networking sites may be the places where kids are likely to hurt each other these days, but those sites, like the bullying, "reinforce pre-existing social relations," according to the report.

Similarly, young people who get in sexual or social trouble online tend to be those who are already at risk offline—doing poorly in school, neglected or abused at home, and/or economically impoverished. According to the Centers for Disease Control and Prevention, a child from a family whose annual income is less than $15,000 is 22 times more likely to suffer sexual abuse than a child whose parents earn more than $30,000.

Sexual or emotional harm precedes risky or harmful on- and offline behavior, rather than the other way around.

Other new research implies that online sexual communication, no matter how much there is, isn't translating into corporeal sex, with either adults or peers. Contrary to popular media depiction of girls and boys going wilder and wilder, La Salle University sociologist and criminal-justice professor Kathleen A. Bogle has found that American teens are more conservative than their elders were at their age. Teen virginity is up and the number of sexual partners is down, she discovered. Only the rate of births to teenage girls has risen in the last few years—a result of declining contraceptive use. This may have something to do with abstinence-only education, which leaves kids reluctant or incompetent when it comes to birth control. Still, the rate of teen births compared to pregnancies always tracks the rate among adult women, and it's doing that now, too.

Like the kids finding adult sex partners in chat rooms, those who fail to protect themselves from pregnancy or sexually transmitted diseases and have their babies young tend to be otherwise at risk emotionally or socially. In other words, kids who are having a rough time in life are having a rough time in virtual life as well. Sexual or emotional harm *precedes* risky or harmful on- and offline behavior, rather than the other way around.

Enter the law—and the injuries of otherwise harmless teenage sexual shenanigans begin. The effects of the ever-stricter sex-crimes laws, which punish ever-younger offenders, are tragic for juveniles. A child pornography conviction—which could come from sending a racy photo of yourself or receiving said photo from a girlfriend or boyfriend—carries far heavier penalties than most hands-on sexual offenses. Even if a juvenile sees no lock-up time, he or she will be forced to register as a sex offender for 10 years or more. The federal Adam Walsh Child Protection Act of 2007 requires that sex offenders as young as 14 register.

The sexual dangers to youth, online or off, may be less than we think.

As documented in such reports as Human Rights Watch's "No Easy Answers: Sex Offender Laws in the U.S." and "Registering Harm: How Sex Offense Registries Fail Youth and Communities" from the Justice Policy Institute, conviction and punishment for a sex crime (a term that includes nonviolent offenses such as consensual teen sex, flashing, and patronizing a prostitute) effectively squashes a minor's chances of getting a college scholarship, serving in the military, securing a good job, finding decent housing, and, in many cases, moving forward with hope or happiness.

The sexual dangers to youth, online or off, may be less than we think. Yet adults routinely conflate friendly sex play with hurtful online behavior. "Teaching Teenagers About Harassment," [a 2009] piece in *The New York Times*, swings between descriptions of consensual photo-swapping and incessant, aggressive texting and Facebook or MySpace rumor- and insult-mongering as if these were similarly motivated—and equally harmful. It quotes the San Francisco–based Family Violence Prevention Fund, which calls sending nude photos "whether it is done under pressure or not" an element of "digital dating violence."

Sober scientific data do nothing to calm such anxieties. Reams of comments flowed into *The New York Times* when it reported Dr. Bogle's findings. "The way TV and MUSIC is promoting sex and explicit content daily and almost on every network," read one typical post, from the aptly named MsKnowledge, "I would have to say this article is completely naive. The streets are talking and there [sic] saying teens and young adults are becoming far more involved in more adult and sexual activities than most ADULTS. Scientific data is a JOKE . . . pay attention to reality and the REAL world will tell you otherwise."

A better-educated interlocutor, NPR's [National Public Radio's] "On the Media" host Brooke Gladstone, defaulted to the same assumption in an interview with one of the Harvard Internet task force members, Family Online Safety Institute CEO Stephen Balkam. What lessons could be drawn from the study's findings? Gladstone asked. "What can be and what should be done to protect kids?"

"There's no silver bullet that's going to solve this issue," Balkam replied. But "far more cooperation has got to happen between law enforcement, industry, the academic community, and we need to understand far better the psychological issues that are at play here."

It's unclear from this exchange what Gladstone believes kids need to be protected from or what issue Balkam is solving. But neither of them came to the logical conclusion of the Harvard study: that we should back off, moderate our fears, and stop thinking of youthful sexual expression as a criminal matter. Still, Balkam wants to call in the cops.

Maybe all that bullying is a mirror of the way adults treat young people minding their own sexual business. Maybe the "issue" is not sex but adults' response to it: the harm we do trying to protect teenagers from themselves.

7

Sexting Is Harmful but Not a Crime

Dahlia Lithwick

Dahlia Lithwick is a contributing editor at Newsweek *and senior editor at* Slate. *Her work has appeared in the* New Republic, Elle, *and the* Washington Post.

As recent cases have shown, child pornography and other criminal laws don't apply to teenagers sending each other erotic photos of themselves, not least of all since it remains unclear who the victims and the perpetrators are. Senders, receivers, and forwarders have been accused, yet swapping photos when nobody feels hurt or abused hardly seems to justify harsh punishment. Some have argued that sending nude photos is an act of violence, but most teenagers think it's fresh and sexy, not a crime. High school students don't have the capacity to make sound decisions all of the time, and their naïveté and lack of foresight should not be grounds for criminal records. Education by adults is a preferable way to treat this new epidemic.

Say you're a middle school principal who has just confiscated a cell phone from a 14-year-old boy, only to discover it contains a nude photo of his 13-year-old girlfriend. Do you: a) call the boy's parents in despair, b) call the girl's parents in despair, or c) call the police? More and more, the answer is d) all of the above. Which could result in criminal charges for both of your students and their eventual designation as sex offenders.

Dahlia Lithwick, "Textual Misconduct," *Slate*, February 14, 2009. The Slate Group, all rights reserved. Used by permission and protected by the Copyright Laws of the United States. The printing, copying, redistribution, or retransmission of the Material without express permission is prohibited.

Sexting is the clever new name for the act of sending, receiving, or forwarding naked photos via your cell phone. I wasn't fully persuaded that America was facing a sexting epidemic, as opposed to a journalists-writing-about-sexting epidemic, until I saw a new survey done by the National Campaign To Prevent Teen and Unplanned Pregnancy. The survey has one teen in five reporting he or she has sent or posted naked photos of himself or herself. Whether all this reflects a new child porn epidemic or just a new iteration of the old shortsighted teen narcissism epidemic remains unclear.

A 15-year-old girl in Ohio and a 14-year-old girl in Michigan were charged with felonies for sending along nude images of themselves to classmates.

Teens Are Facing Criminal Charges

Last month [January 2009] three girls (ages 14 or 15) in Greensburg, Pa., were charged with disseminating child pornography for sexting their boyfriends. The boys who received the images were charged with possession. A teenager in Indiana faces felony obscenity charges for sending a picture of his genitals to female classmates. A 15-year-old girl in Ohio and a 14-year-old girl in Michigan were charged with felonies for sending along nude images of themselves to classmates. Some of these teens have pleaded guilty to lesser charges; others have not. If convicted, these young people may have to register as sex offenders, in some cases for a decade or two. Similar charges have been filed in cases in Alabama, Connecticut, Florida, New Jersey, New York, Texas, Utah, and Wisconsin.

One quick clue that the criminal justice system is probably not the best venue for addressing the sexting crisis? A survey of the charges brought in the cases reflects that—depending on the jurisdiction—prosecutors have charged the *senders* of smutty photos, the *recipients* of smutty photos, those who *save* the smutty photos, and the hapless *forwarders* of smutty photos with the same crime: child pornography. Who is the victim here and who is the perpetrator? Everybody and nobody.

There may be an argument for police intervention in cases that involve a genuine threat or cyber-bullying, such as a recent Massachusetts incident in which the picture of a naked 14-year-old girl was allegedly sent to more than 100 cell phones, or a New York case involving a group of boys who turned a nude photo of a 15-year-old girl into crude animations and PowerPoint presentations. But are such cases really the same as the cases in which tipsy teen girls send their boyfriends naughty Valentine's Day pictures?

Child pornography laws intended to protect children should not be used to prosecute and then label children as sex offenders.

The argument for hammering every such case seems to be that allowing nude images of yourself to go public may have serious consequences, so let's nip it in the bud by charging kids with felonies, which will assuredly have serious consequences. In the Pennsylvania case, for instance, a police captain explained that the charges were brought because "it's very dangerous. Once it's on a cell phone, that cell phone can be put on the Internet where everyone in the world can get access to that juvenile picture." The argument that we must prosecute kids as the producers and purveyors of kiddie porn because they are too dumb to understand that their seemingly innocent acts can hurt them goes beyond paternalism. Child pornography laws intended to protect children should not be used to prosecute and then label children as sex offenders.

Children Are Not Sex Offenders

Consider the way in which school districts have reacted to the uptick in sexting. Have they cracked down on the epidemic?

Confiscated cell phones? Launched widespread Lolita drag-nets? No, many now simply prohibit students from bringing cell phones to school. This doesn't stop students from sexting. It just stops them from being caught. How bad can sexting really be if schools are enacting what amounts to a don't-ask-don't-tell policy?

Parents can forget that their kids may be as tech-savvy as Bill Gates but as gullible as Bambi. At some level, teens understand that once their image reaches someone else's cell phone, what happened in Vegas is unlikely to stay there. The National Campaign To Prevent Teen and Unplanned Pregnancy survey suggests 25 percent of teen girls and 33 percent of teen boys report seeing naked images originally sent to someone else. Yet even in the age of the Internet, young people fail to appreciate that their naked pictures want to roam free.

The same survey showed that teens can be staggeringly naive in another way: Twenty percent have posted a naked photo of themselves despite the fact that 71 percent of those asked understand that doing so can have serious negative consequences. Understanding the consequences of risky behavior but engaging in it anyhow? Smells like teen spirit to me.

If we are worried about the poor girls pressured into exposing themselves, why are we treating them more harshly than the boys?

The real problem with criminalizing teen sexting as a form of child pornography is that the great majority of these kids are not predators and have no intention of producing or purveying kiddie porn. They think they're being brash and sexy, in the manner of brash, sexy Americans everywhere: by being undressed. And while some of the reaction to the sexting epidemic reflects legitimate concerns about children as sex objects, some highlights pernicious legal stereotypes and fallacies. A recent [2009] *New York Times* article about online harassment, for instance, quotes the Family Violence Prevention Fund, a nonprofit domestic violence awareness group, saying that the sending of nude pictures, even if done voluntarily, constitutes "digital dating violence." But is one in five teens truly participating in an act of violence?

Peer Pressure Is a Real Problem

Many other experts insist the sexting trend hurts teen girls more than boys, fretting that they feel "pressured" to take and send naked photos. Yet the girls in the Pennsylvania case were charged with "manufacturing, disseminating or possessing child pornography" while the boys were merely charged with possession. This disparity seems increasingly common. If we are worried about the poor girls pressured into exposing themselves, why are we treating them more harshly than the boys?

In a thoughtful essay in the *American Prospect* Online, Judith Levine, author of *Harmful to Minors: The Perils of Protecting Children From Sex* examines the dangers lurking online for children and concludes that the harms of old-fashioned online bullying—the sort of teasing and ostracism that led [13-year-old] Megan Meier to kill herself [in 2006] after being tormented on MySpace—far outweigh the dangers of online sexual material. Judging from the sexting prosecutions in Pennsylvania and Ohio last year, it's clear the criminal justice system is too blunt an instrument to resolve a problem that reflects more about the volatile combination of teens and technology than some national cyber-crime spree. Parents need to remind their teens that a dumb moment can last a lifetime in cyberspace. Judges and prosecutors need to understand that a lifetime of cyber-humiliation shouldn't be grounds for a very real and possibly lifelong criminal record.

8

Punishment for Sexting Teens Might Be Too Harsh

Dionne Searcey

Dionne Searcey is a reporter for the Wall Street Journal.

In 2009, Wyoming County, Pennsylvania, district attorney George Skumanick Jr. put parents and teenagers on alert. He threatened to charge a group of teenagers who had engaged in sexting with violations of pornography laws. The American Civil Liberties Union and many parents strongly oppose Skumanick's stance and argued that such punishments were unreasonable. A court case such as this, parents and students believe, would harm and expose teenagers much more than the circulation of suggestive photos.

The group of anxious parents crowded around District Attorney George Skumanick Jr. as he sat behind a table in a courtroom here [in Tunkhannock, Pa.] and presented them with an ultimatum.

Photos of their semi-nude or scantily clad teenage daughters were stacked before him. Mr. Skumanick said the images had been discovered on cellphones confiscated at the local high school. They could either enlist their kids in an education program or have the teens face felony charges of child pornography. "We could have just arrested them but we didn't," said Mr. Skumanick in an interview.

Dionne Searcey, "A Lawyer, Some Teens and a Fight over 'Sexting,'" *The Wall Street Journal*, April 21, 2009. Copyright © by Dow Jones and Company, Inc. Reproduced by permission.

An Alarming Trend

The practice of teens taking naked photos of themselves and sending them to friends via cellphones, called "sexting," has alarmed parents, school officials and prosecutors nationwide, who fear the photos could end up on the Internet or in the hands of sexual predators. In a handful of cases, authorities have resorted to what one parent here called "the nuclear weapon of sex charges"—child pornography.

But some legal experts say that here in Wyoming County, Pa., Mr. Skumanick has expanded the definition of sexting to such an extent he could be setting a dangerous precedent. He has threatened to charge kids who appeared in photos, but who didn't send them, as well as at least one girl who was photographed wearing a bathing suit. One of the accused is 11 years old.

Many prosecutors say pornography laws should be used to protect children from adults, not from other children.

"The whole tawdry episode seems to call for a little parental guidance and a pop-gun approach, not a Howitzer [heavy artillery] approach with a felony prosecution," said Louis Natali, a law professor at Temple University.

The sexting case in Tunkhannock is being closely tracked by juvenile-justice authorities. Many prosecutors say pornography laws should be used to protect children from adults, not from other children. In some cases, teens could end up listed on sex registries if convicted of child pornography. Others say that if charges are made, they should be limited to kids who actually distribute the photos.

Calling for Moderation

Last month [March 2009], the American Civil Liberties Union [ACLU] and a group of parents sued Mr. Skumanick in federal court in Scranton, Pa., alleging he violated the freedom-of-expression rights of three teenage girls. The ACLU also says that Mr. Skumanick is interfering with their parents' rights to raise them as they see fit.

Others say Mr. Skumanick is giving the teens an opportunity to avoid charges, which he could have filed immediately. Mr. Skumanick says he plans to appeal and says he didn't have to offer the education courses as a way out. "We thought we were being progressive."

Some see Mr. Skumanick's alternative of offering classes as appealing. "You don't want to tag them with a scarlet letter for the rest of their life," says Shannon Edmonds, a staff attorney at the Texas District and County Attorneys Association, about charging teens with sex crimes.

Sexting came into the spotlight in this rural town, population 1,900, in October [2008]. A female student in the Tunkhannock High School cafeteria saw a boy scrolling through his cellphone and spotted a nude photo of herself, according to Mr. Skumanick. When the girl became upset, the school took the phone and called the police who, in turn, handed it to the district attorney's office.

The girl, Jessica Logan, had sent nude photos of herself to her boyfriend and later hanged herself after being harassed by schoolmates when the boy allegedly sent the images to his friends.

Mr. Skumanick, 47, has been district attorney for the past 20 years here in his boyhood home. He says he was troubled by the photo, and what worried him most was an incident in Ohio where the mother of a teenager blamed sexting for her daughter's suicide last year [2008]. The girl, Jessica Logan, had sent nude photos of herself to her boyfriend and later hanged herself after being harassed by schoolmates when the boy allegedly sent the images to his friends.

As Mr. Skumanick contemplated what to do, the school turned up several other phones with nude or semi-nude photos of students. One showed an image of a 17-year-old girl in a towel wrapped just below her breasts. The girl, who asked not to be identified, said she sent the photo to her boyfriend about a year ago to make him jealous when she heard he was interested in another girl. "It was just stupid," she said in an interview.

Photos Come Back to Haunt Senders

Another confiscated phone had photos of a 17-year-old girl that she described in an interview as "semi-nude pictures, underwear and stuff like that." The girl, who took the photos herself, was debating whether to send them to her boyfriend when a teacher took the phone.

Mr. Skumanick thought he had enough evidence to charge them as juveniles on pornography violations—not just for sending the photos, but for appearing in them, too.

With the help of school officials, Mr. Skumanick convened a series of assemblies, from fifth-graders to seniors. For the youngest students, he asked them to conjure how they would feel if their grandparents saw a photo of them that is "not nice." He warned the older students that sexting could damage their college or job prospects and could result in felony charges.

At one of the assemblies, a student interrupted and accused Mr. Skumanick of trying to ruin the teens' lives. "This isn't a debate," Mr. Skumanick told the senior boy, who was escorted out of the auditorium.

Mr. Skumanick also worked with area youth officials to offer the teens a class in lieu of charges. Patrick Rushton, education manager at the Wyoming County Victims Resource Center, culled course outlines for both boys and girls from educational Web sites on sexual harassment and violence. His curriculum included material on "what it means to be a girl in today's society" and a poem, "Phenomenal Women," by Maya Angelou.

On Feb. 5, with the course outline mostly in order, Mr. Skumanick sent a letter to parents of the students involved, saying their children had been "identified in a police investigation involving the possession and/or dissemination of child pornography." The letter summoned the parents to a Feb. 12 meeting at the Wyoming County Courthouse.

A Matter of Interpretation

MaryJo Miller was dumbstruck when she opened her letter, which targeted her daughter, Marissa. Mr. Skumanick later told her he had a photo of Marissa that showed her from the waist up wearing a bra.

Marissa and her mother say the photo was snapped at a slumber party more than two years ago when Marissa was 12. Neither Marissa nor her mother knows how it got circulated but they don't see the photo as explicit. "It was like an old grandma bra. Nothing skimpy," says Marissa.

Marissa and her parents joined a group of about 50 others at the courthouse. Before showing the photos, Mr. Skumanick explained his offer to the crowd, answering one father's question affirmatively, that—yes—a girl in a bathing suit could be subjected to criminal charges because she was posed "provocatively."

Mr. Skumanick told them he could have simply charged the kids. Instead, he gave them two weeks to decide: take the class or face charges.

He then told the parents and teens to line up if they wanted to view the photos, which were printed out onto index cards. As the 17-year-old who took semi-nude self-portraits waited in line, she realized that Mr. Skumanick and other investigators had viewed the pictures. When the adults began to crowd around Mr. Skumanick, the 17-year-old worried they could see her photo and recalls she said, "I think the worst punishment is knowing that all you old guys saw me naked. I just think you guys are all just perverts."

Mr. Skumanick dismisses the criticism, saying that no one could see photos of teens who weren't their own children.

In the end, parents enrolled 14 teens in the course. But the parents of three other girls, including Marissa Miller, recruited the ACLU's help to sue Mr. Skumanick. At a hearing March 26, [2009,] a federal judge indicated he thought the girls may be successful in their suit and temporarily blocked Mr. Skumanick from filing charges, pending a June hearing.

9

Sexting Should Not Be Prosecuted Under Existing Laws

Julie Hilden

Julie Hilden, a Yale Law School graduate, formerly practiced First Amendment law in Washington, D.C., and has been writing about First Amendment issues ever since. She's a columnist for FindLaw.com and has published the novel 3.

Child pornography laws were not meant to include sexting, nor were laws against contributing to the delinquency of a minor, known as "contributing" statutes. Before prosecutors and judges apply irrelevant laws to teenagers with no criminal intent or awareness, they should investigate why society is outraged by sexting, and what probable punishment would fit this alleged crime. Otherwise, the legal system will fail teenagers' needs miserably and group them together with hardened criminals, jeopardizing their futures. While society is concerned that nude pictures might end up in the wrong hands, this concern should not be turned into a denial of teen sexuality and its current expression. Sexting might not be safe, but it is no crime.

In a recent [2009] column . . . , I took issue with an attempt to prosecute teenagers' "sexting"—that is, the practice of sending semi-nude or nude photos of each other via cellphone—under anti-child-pornography laws. The column was prompted by a Pennsylvania D.A.'s [district attorney's] threat

Julie Hilden, "Why Sexting Should Not Be Prosecuted as 'Contributing to the Delinquency of a Minor,'" FindLaw.com, May 13, 2009. Copyright © 2009 by FindLaw. Reproduced by permission.

to prosecute three teenage girls who had "sexted" photos of themselves, in which they were wearing only bras and no shirts, or were topless, to fellow students.

As I noted, the D.A's threat sparked a suit from the ACLU [American Civil Liberties Union]. The suit sought to counteract the "chilling effect" of the prosecutors' threat upon the exercise of these and other teens' free speech rights. The ACLU pointed out, as well, that child pornography is defined by law as depicting sexual activity, or depicting the lascivious display of the genitals—and the girls' photos simply did not qualify.

The Dangers of Appropriating Existing Laws

However, child pornography laws are not the only laws that have been invoked to try to target sexting. In Ohio, earlier this year [2009], there was also an attempt to use contributing-to-the-delinquency-of-a-minor laws against teens alleged to have engaged in sexting.

Putting teen sexters on sex-offender registries alongside hardened criminals could haunt the teens for life, and cause them to be confused with rapists and child pornographers.

But these laws, too, are inapposite [inappropriate], and their application to sexting is potentially dangerous—as I will explain. Here, too, authorities are trying to shoehorn the practice of sexting within the bounds of prior laws that are inapposite—a strategy that poses the danger of both free speech violations and unfair and disproportionate punishments for teens.

There is no shortcut here: Legislators need to write new laws—and/or schools must write new policies—regarding sexting that are specifically geared toward the peculiarities of the practice as it exists among teenagers today. "Sexting" should not become a trap for the unwary; it should be addressed in a rational, consistent way, and in a way that eschews [shuns] old categories to recognize its unique nature. Teens should also have clear prior notice of what they cannot do, and of what will happen to them if they break the rules.

"Contributing" Statutes

In Ohio, earlier this year, two teens were charged with contributing to the delinquency of a minor after an assistant principal discovered them apparently "sexting" an explicit photo of a fifteen-year-old girl. The case was one factor inspiring Ohio state representatives to seek to redefine sexting by juveniles as a first-degree misdemeanor, partly in order to keep young culprits off sex-offender registries yet still bring their actions within the criminal law.

There should be no question that it was wrong for Ohio prosecutors to invoke the contributing-to-the-delinquency-of-a-minor laws in this context—for a number of reasons.

First, the legislators' concern was an important one: Putting teen sexters on sex-offender registries alongside hardened criminals could haunt the teens for life, and cause them to be confused with rapists and child pornographers.

Second, such statutes are plainly intended to apply primarily, if not exclusively, to adults, and the penalties are tailored accordingly. Indeed, some such statutes are expressly limited to apply only to parents, guardians, and others in a caretaking relationship with the child, and thus are more or less limited to adults (although teen babysitters or older siblings could conceivably fall within such laws too). But Ohio's law is broader, referring simply to "persons" as well as to caretakers.

Third—as a law school classmate of mine once argued, very persuasively—such statutes are so vague on their face that they should be held to be invalid under the constitutional void-for-vagueness doctrine. Granted, courts have repeatedly held to the contrary, but I believe that's because this is an area where a concern for protecting children at all costs has led to a series of mistaken rulings that ignore clear constitutional principle. Such rulings may seem understandable, but they make constitutional law incoherent. Even the heinous crime of child rape must be, and is, carefully defined by law—yet "contributing" statutes, which can apply to comparatively minor transgressions, need not be? If the goal is to protect children from crime, the law seems to have it backward.

Generally, under the void-for-vagueness doctrine, criminal statutes—because of the gravity of the penalties they impose—must be quite clear about the conduct they describe. That is part of the Constitution's right to due process. But "contributing" statutes are extremely unclear—and intentionally so, for they function as a legal catch-all. When more specific criminal statutes do not apply, "contributing" statutes are used to round up the usual suspects—typically, adults who are often seen hanging out with teens, and who have not yet committed any other crime, but who seem like they might well have bad intentions or be "bad influences."

Vague Laws Invite Abuse

Readers may ask: So what? What's wrong with putting these apparent bad apples away before they ruin kids' lives? One answer is that like loitering statutes and the law allowing cars to be pulled over on a police officer's whim, "contributing" statutes are prone to misuse. Such statutes, by their nature, may be invoked when crime is suspected, but not proven—betraying our system's tenet of "guilt beyond a reasonable doubt." And, in this instance, the problem may not just be one of proof: The crime may not be able to be proven because, in fact, it was never committed in the first place.

Moreover, racism or other forms of discrimination may be behind the application of "contributing" statutes—with police claiming to be motivated only by a concern for teens, but really being motivated by something very different. Imagine that an African-American teen is hanging out with seventeen-year-old white kids in the suburbs. He's a friend, but police suspect he's a drug-dealer. Unable to prove the drug-dealing, they tell the African-American teen to get lost or else be charged with "contributing" under a statute like Ohio's.

It's important to recall ... that the blunt instrument of the criminal law is not the only weapon here. School and parental penalties still remain as options.

For all these reasons, the last thing we need is to extend the reach of already-worrisome "contributing" criminal statutes, into the new area of sexting.

It's important to recall, too, that the blunt instrument of the criminal law is not the only weapon here. School and parental penalties still remain as options.

Teens' Consent and Free Speech Rights

Finally, there is a special feature of sexting that makes prosecuting minors under "contributing" statutes for sexting especially inappropriate: "Contributing" statutes don't look to the consent of the minor. That is probably because, with respect to virtually all of the conduct that the statutes' drafters envisioned as delinquent, the minor's consent is immaterial. Indeed, "contributing" laws' animating concern is that someone may be getting a minor to consent to something that he or she might not consent to do, absent the bad influence of another.

In contrast, consent should matter greatly when it comes to sexting—at least, sexting among roughly same-age students. . . . Large age differences may eventually negate consent, but as with statutory-rape laws, it seems clear that a

Romeo-and-Juliet sexting exception should apply at some point—creating a safe harbor for same-age couples and consensual sexting.

It would be absurd, for instance, for two sixteen-year-olds who are dating to be deemed criminals because each sent a nude photo of him- or herself to the other, while meaning for the photo to be kept entirely private. Teenagers do have First Amendment rights—and, with the exception of obscene (and in this context, obscene-as-to-minors) speech, sexual speech is protected.

Teens' nonconsensual forwarding of other teens' photos, of course, is a much harder scenario—but media accounts of sexting still tend to focus more on teen sexuality, than on the real issue: forwarding without consent. In the absence of a large age gap, it is forwarding without consent that should be the law's primary—and often, only—concern.

And in this area, we need to start asking and answering difficult questions—questions that make a real effort to choose a rational place to put unconsented sexting on the broad continuum of moral blame and punishment, and to address it in a way that deters and punishes it, but also takes into account the youth of offenders.

> *Teenagers do have First Amendment rights—and, with the exception of obscene speech . . . , sexual speech is protected.*

Far Beyond Traditional Bullying

The question is complicated: Unconsented sexting seems partly like bullying, to which it often leads, when the photos' subject is later humiliated in person by peers, or receives nasty phone calls or texts. But unconsented sexting also has a communal aspect, when photos are very widely forwarded among a large school community, that even group bullying rarely attains. As with file-sharing, we see "cat out of the bag" problems with sexting, and a sexted photo might go viral, reaching viewers well beyond the physical confines of a particular school.

Before we decide whether sexting should be a crime, a tort, or neither, and how to punish it, we need a better sense of why it has caused such an outcry in the first place.

Moreover, to look only at the bullying component of un-consented sexting would be to ignore its obvious sexual com-ponent. Sexism plays a role here too—a boy who is bullied, or who is the victim of unconsented sexting, may be told to "man up," whereas girls—like those in the Pennsylvania case—who are comfortable with their own sexuality may be told by the prosecutor, as those girls were, to take a class on "what it means to be a girl in today's society."

To complicate matters further, there seems to be no ques-tion that the current generation's sexual mores are somewhat different from those of generations past—but how, and how much? Should student councils weigh in on sexting incidents before school principals take action—including actions like referring culprits for prosecution? If they don't, there may be sexting prosecutions where no harm was done or meant.

Before we decide whether sexting should be a crime, a tort [a civil violation enabling a victim to sue for damages], or neither, and how to punish it, we need a better sense of why it has caused such an outcry in the first place. Is it because we don't want to acknowledge teen sexuality, because we are un-comfortable with teen speech rights, or because we are furious about teen bullying and humiliation—or perhaps all of the above?

10

Exposure to Pornography Is Linked to Sexting

Penny Marshall

Penny Marshall has been a television news foreign correspondent since the 1980s and has reported from eastern Europe and the former Soviet Union. She is a regular presenter and writer for BBC Radio 4, a visiting professor of journalism at London's City University, and a contributor to many newspapers and magazines.

Teenagers today are obsessed with watching and creating pornography, and the practice of sexting is a new and dangerous symptom. Teens post nude pictures of themselves on social networking sites, and boys bully girls into sending them revealing pictures. But the dangers are manifold and in extreme cases can lead to harassment, a criminal record, and bullying so severe that it results in suicide. Believing that the content of their images is private, teenagers are exposing themselves to strangers on the Internet and risk being contacted by predators. Sexting is especially prevalent among children from well-to-do backgrounds, many of whom own computers and electronic gadgets that make it easy to create and access such images. If society does not interfere, many teenagers might do irreparable harm to their lives and careers.

Like a real porn star, Becky is heavily made up and lying naked on the bed as the camera flashes. She could be just another glamorous model as she poses provocatively with

Penny Marshall, "Generation Sexting: What Teenage Girls Really Get Up to on the Internet Should Chill Every Parent," *Daily Mail*, March 18, 2009. Copyright © 2009 by Solo Syndication. Reprinted with permission.

practised moves. But she isn't. Shockingly, Becky is just 17 and still at school. She's filming herself in a friend's bedroom in a large, detached house in leafy suburbia as her schoolfriends party downstairs.

Becky has not been coerced into this degrading behaviour. She is posing on her own, taking photographs of herself not for profit—but for attention. Welcome to the deeply alarming new world of privileged British teenagers who have a growing obsession with pornography.

A Shocking Discovery

I discovered this trend—one which will horrify parents everywhere—during a BBC Radio 4 investigation into online pornography.

As a mother of three daughters aged 15, 14 and 12, I am well aware of the pressures children face online, and the problems adults confront trying to help them navigate their way through them.

Indeed, it was my concerns about my children's online exposure that made me take a closer look at this secretive teenage social world.

It's a world—as I was to discover—where boys often boast about the size of their manhood and their ability to drink alcohol, while girls flaunt themselves shamelessly, apeing the adult behaviour they see around them on TV and in magazines.

My guide into this disturbing universe was a pretty A-level student. I'd come to talk to her and a group of sixth-formers [high school juniors and seniors]—boys as well as girls—at their prestigious school about the impact that *watching* pornography may be having on today's youngsters.

I certainly was not prepared to hear they were also *producing* it.

Talking to leading academics, I had already found out that our children are watching a great deal of porn online—some of it hard-core—and that its long-term effects could be damaging. I had also discovered that they are watching it at a very early age, sometimes as young as eight, as the internet beams it into their bedrooms.

Even taking into account the obvious fact that teenagers are prone to exaggeration, it became alarmingly clear to me that most of these teenagers were not exaggerating their involvement with pornography.

'Everyone makes porn—more people than you would expect,' an articulate sixth-former told me matter-of-factly, before describing how her 17-year-old friend had photographed herself.

This girl had used her mobile phone to capture her provocative poses and sent them on afterwards, sometimes unsolicited, to boys—a disturbing trend that has been dubbed 'sexting'.

Exposing Oneself to Others

'Over the holidays, I went to a party with people from my old school and one of the girls was on her bed with nothing on. She had loads and loads of makeup on, so you could see that she'd thought about it.'

This girl had used her mobile phone to capture her provocative poses and sent them on afterwards, sometimes unsolicited, to boys—a disturbing trend that has been dubbed 'sexting'.

'I'm not sure exactly who she sent the photos to, but one of the boys at this school now has it.'

I asked how usual it was for girls to pose provocatively, or even pornographically.

'Oh, it's really common,' she told me brightly. 'Most people who have got a social networking account will have a provocative picture.'

Provocative, I learned from talking to teenagers and looking at their pages, means scantily clad or semi-naked (usually in underwear), sometimes posing sexually, and always pouting suggestively.

Several girls told me they were often pestered to send explicit photos of themselves to boys.

'And there's nudity,' the girl continued. 'And it's not normally the sluttier girls who do this—it's more likely to be the shy type of girl who wants to be popular.

'They're the ones who will get easily swayed by boys, because boys want to see them naked, and they think that if they show them themselves naked . . .'

Several girls told me they were often pestered to send explicit photos of themselves to boys.

'I said no to that,' one confided. 'But I know girls who give in really easily.'

An Illegal Habit

For the Radio 4 programme, I spoke to children from a range of public and state schools. It is certainly not the case that this behaviour is being perpetrated by those from a deprived background or those who lack intelligence. In fact, it's the privileged, supposedly brightest youngsters who are most at risk.

'What some of today's youngsters are doing is, by any civilised, contemporary standards, obscene,' says John Carr of the UK's [United Kingdom's] Children's Charities' Coalition on Internet Safety.

'It also happens to be illegal. It's a genuinely new problem which is the result of the emergence of new technology together with an increasing cultural tolerance of pornography.

'It's horrifying, and we are only now becoming aware of the full extent of the problem.

'Publishing any photograph of a child—that's anyone under 18—which is of a sexual nature is illegal. So children who put pornographic photographs of themselves online or share the material via their mobile phones are, technically, breaking the law.'

So far, 90 children in the UK have been cautioned as a result of posting sexual material of themselves or their underage friends online or on their mobile phones.

This is the first generation to become sexually active with the internet, and the internet is playing its part in the process—sometimes with horrifying consequences.

Pornography and Internet Access

'There was a notorious case not so long ago where a 13-year-old girl took a picture of herself touching herself in an intimate sexual manner,' says Mr Carr.

'She sent it to her boyfriend, who thought it would be smart to send it to five of his friends. Within a few hours, the police reckon, it was on about 1,000 different screens.

'The police managed to trace the girl through the school because she was wearing her uniform. They treated the case very seriously; but in the end they didn't prosecute her.'

In the U.S., teenagers filming themselves having sex or posing provocatively are considered to be a legitimate target for prosecution by the authorities.

One of the teenage boys I spoke to described the online humiliation of a young friend.

'It can really backfire on you, that sort of stuff,' he told me. 'Recently, a friend of mine broke up with her boyfriend. The boy was very upset and, as a result, sent a video of her to all her friends.

'Obviously she's very upset about this. I think that this sort of thing happens very often nowadays.'

In the U.S., teenagers filming themselves having sex or posing provocatively are considered to be a legitimate target for prosecution by the authorities.

Dr Samuel McQuade, from the Rochester Institute of Technology in New York, is one of the leading world experts on internet safety. He is alarmed by the rapid rise in what he calls 'peer pseudo-pornography'.

'In Connecticut last autumn [2008], a decision was made to prosecute a 12-year-old girl for allegedly having taken pictures of herself without clothes on and sending them to boys of a similar age,' says Dr McQuade.

'And this is not an isolated case. In the U.S., there have been other children who have been prosecuted. And empirical data suggests that hundreds, perhaps thousands, and maybe even more, are getting involved in this.

'Children, who are not educated about the implications of this type of behaviour, are slipping into these kinds of activities. They are egged on by their friends.'

Generational Gap Widening

Today's digital youth culture is not a place for the faint-hearted. As I talked to teenagers, I began to realise that there was more than a digital divide separating us.

What I see as soft pornography, totally inappropriate and disturbing for children to make or pose for, some of them see as harmless, if provocative, teenage fun.

When boys told me they had been sent pictures by girls of themselves posing topless and even naked, it seemed to most of them a bit of a joke—until I told them that looking at such material of underage girls was illegal.

In the past year, there have been at least two cases where police have been called into schools after footage of pupils performing sex acts has been discovered on their phones. One involved youngsters as young as 13. One of the teenagers I spoke to acknowledged that filming sex sessions does happen.

'It's nothing to do with how you are brought up,' she said. 'It's just out there now.'

David Wright is a leading online child protection officer who was called in to investigate computer use in schools after the Soham murders [two 10-year-old British girls were murdered by a school caretaker in 2002]. He tours the South-West of England talking to parents, teachers and pupils.

He believes that it's often the most well-off children—those with laptops in their bedrooms, digital cameras and wireless access in their homes—who are the most at risk.

'Up to 39 per cent of parents say they have never spoken to their children about how the internet should be used,' he says.

'Police forces tell us that children at most risk online are 11- to 14-year-olds from professional families, all with internet access in their bedroom.

'You might not necessarily classify those as society's most vulnerable, but they're the ones that the police are dealing with on a weekly basis.'

Children of the Well-to-Do at Risk

It usually starts at around 11 or 12 years of age. Parents who buy their children computers to help them study at secondary school often recoil in horror as they see them pout, preen and pose for that first all-important 'profile picture' for their networking site.

These pictures are then uploaded to illustrate their pages on networking sites such as Facebook and Bebo. Though these sites have a minimum age requirement of 13, many parents, and most sites, appear unable to enforce this.

And then there's the avalanche of pornographic material beamed onto every computer screen unless it is actively blocked. According to one U.S. software producer, 25 per cent of all the daily search engine requests are for pornographic material, and it's estimated that one in ten of all websites is pornographic.

Much of the internet's professionally produced porn is available free. What was once the subject of an obscenity trial is now just two clicks away.

Some of the children I spoke to—girls as well as boys—were accessing porn.

Disturbingly, some were deliberately seeking out some of the most stomach-churning material I have ever heard of—material I hope I shall never see—and sending links to each other to view it. As a joke.

It was material that made even this hardened foreign correspondent feel ill. While some of the worse stuff, involving extreme sexual violence, has been outlawed following a change in the law in January [2009], much of it remains free-to-view and perfectly legal.

In the light of this, the 'sexualisation' of young teenage and even pre-teen girls through clothes, videos and music lyrics, and a possible link with sexual abuse and violence, is to be the focus of a fact-finding review ordered by the Home Secretary [the cabinet-level minister in charge of British domestic affairs].

If children see this material around them, is it any wonder that they ape it when left to create their own content?

Search for the words 'porn star' on the popular networking site Bebo and the results include the profiles of more than 21,000 members. That represents the number of children and adults using those words on their sites.

Pornography Is Pervasive

Geoff Barton is the headmaster of King Edward VI School in Bury St Edmunds. He believes that children are living in a society with far too low a tolerance threshold for pornography.

Children are being sexualised far too young, he believes. This is contributing to the emergence of their online sexual behaviour.

'Any school that says it is not an issue for them is putting their heads in the sand,' he says.

'Parents are at a loss. We need to rewrite the parenting handbook.'

At one of his school assemblies, their head of IT [information technology] reproduced some of the more provocative but clothed online images he could find of some of their pupils in order to shock them.

'We removed their heads from the pictures first to protect their identities, but they knew who they were,' says Geoff Barton.

'What they are doing is very, very reckless and dangerous. But it's all part of the "pornification" of a generation for whom the language and imagery of porn is used to sell everything.

'In a world where even an ad for Pot Noodle [a snack food] has to be banned for its sexual suggestiveness, how can you expect children to behave?

'It's as if we've decided to give up on the traditional demarcation between adult life and childhood. In the process, we've ditched some of our adult responsibilities.

'We need to teach children how to behave online, how to navigate the architecture of the net.'

There is so much to lose for these youngsters—from their dignity to their job prospects.

Endangering Future Careers

John Carr says teenagers who behave inappropriately or obscenely and post their material online could do lasting and irreversible damage to their future chances of success.

'Children feel invincible online. They believe the material they are producing is private. But they are wrong on both counts.

'We've had documented accounts of employers, and universities and colleges, trawling the net looking for information about prospective candidates. This behaviour can have long-lasting effects. What goes online stays online—for ever.'

There is so much to lose for these youngsters—from their dignity to their job prospects. So much, in fact, that every parent reading this should check their child's social networking site. If they won't let you take a look at their photos, ask them why.

But perhaps the most precious thing of all has been lost already. And that is our children's innocence.

11

Sexting Is a Symptom of American Culture

Tracy Clark-Flory

Tracy Clark-Flory is a staff writer at Salon.com, where she blogs for the Broadsheet section and writes feature stories. One of her essays was included in the anthology Best Sex Writing of 2009.

Sexting has become a kind of self-expression in sync with our highly sexualized and pornographic culture. With the rise of the Internet and smartphones, provocative and pornographic imagery is but a click away, and it becomes increasingly harder for parents to explain to their children where the line between desirable and undesirable sexuality is, especially in a culture that has no such clearly defined boundaries. It is normal for teens to experiment with sexuality, but in an exhibitionistic, highly sexualized culture, young people's online expressions of sexuality can put them in danger—of being humiliated, blackmailed, targeted by pedophiles, or accused of transmitting child pornography.

The photographs show three naked underage girls posing lasciviously for the camera. The perps who took the pictures were busted in Greensburg, Pa., and charged with manufacturing, disseminating and possessing child pornography— and so were their subjects. That's because they are one and the same.

It all started when the girls, ages 14 and 15, decided to take nudie cellphone snapshots of themselves. Then, maybe

Tracy Clark-Flory, "The New Pornographers," Salon.com, February 20, 2009. This article first appeared in Salon.com, at http://www.Salon.com. An online version remains in the Salon archives. Reprinted with permission.

feeling dizzy from the rush of wielding their feminine wiles, the trio text-messaged the photos to some friends at Greensburg-Salem High School. When one of the students' cellphones was confiscated at school, the photos were discovered. Police opened an investigation and, in addition to the girls being indicted as kiddie pornographers, three boys who received the pictures were slammed with charges of child porn possession. All but one ultimately accepted lesser misdemeanor charges.

Teens will, as they always have, experiment with their sexuality.

New Legal Challenges

"Sexting," where kids trade X-rated pictures via text message, has made headlines recently after a rash of cases in which child pornography charges have been brought not against dangerous pedophiles but hormonally haywire teenagers— potentially leaving them branded sex offenders for life. Just last week [in February 2009], there came news that a middle-school boy in Falmouth, Mass., might face child porn charges for sending a naughty photo of his 13-year-old girlfriend to five buddies, who are also being investigated. There's been plenty of outrage to go around: Some parents are angry to see teens criminalized for simply being sexual, while others find the raunchy shots pornographic, another blinking neon sign of moral decay in a "Girls Gone Wild" era. In both cases, it amounts to a tug of war between teenagers' entitled sense of sexual autonomy and society's desire to protect them.

It's rather stunning that in the same age of the Pussycat Dolls, Disney starlets' sexy photo scandals, Slut-o-ween costumes for kids and preteen push-up bras and thongs, teenagers are being charged with child porn possession for having photographs of their own naked bodies. That noise you hear? It's the grating sound of cultural dissonance.

Judging Teenagers' Sexuality

According to these recent interpretations of the law, a curious teenage girl who embarks on an "Our Bodies, Ourselves" journey of vaginal self-discovery, and simply replaces a hand mirror with a digital camera, is a kiddie pornographer. The same goes for the boy who memorializes his raging boner or the post-pubescent girl who takes test shots of herself practicing the porn star poses she has studied online. Theoretically, this is true regardless of whether they share the pictures with anyone, and if they do share them, they could be additionally charged with peddling child porn.

There are plenty of examples of the moral and legal gray areas created as technology broadens our behaviors: cyber-cheating, MySpace bullying, online gossip, upskirting [a form of voyeurism], employers' Web snooping. When it comes to "sexting," though, the potentially damaging implications—for child pornography law, free speech and kids' sexuality—are abundant. And it's not going away any time soon. A recent online poll found that 20 percent of teens have shared nude or semi-nude photos or videos of themselves, the majority with a boyfriend or girlfriend. (Sure, voluntary polls tend to be self-selecting, but the results seem obvious, maybe even understated.) Teens will, as they always have, experiment with their sexuality. But at a time when free hardcore porn is ubiquitous, technology is cheap and the Internet is a comfortable channel for expression and experimentation, is it really any surprise that this is a generation of amateur pornographers?

It certainly isn't to 20-somethings like myself who came of age during the Internet's youth. By the time I was 14, I had seen my share of online porn and late-night HBO and made frequent use of the phrase "U wanna cyber?" in early AOL chat rooms. In high school in Berkeley, Calif., at least two student sex tapes were rumored to be making the rounds. I didn't have a cellphone camera or a webcam, thank god—though I did have a Polaroid camera, which, to be sure, my longtime boyfriend and I toyed around with.

Today's teens have an entirely different notion of privacy than past generations.

Becoming a Part of the Sexual Culture

This is all part of how kids initiate themselves into our sexual culture long before they actually have sex. At one time, that meant a boy would flip through his father's stash of *Playboys* and a girl would try on her mother's ample bra. For me, it meant privately mimicking the stripper moves I had seen on TV and having online chats with people who occasionally turned out to be aging pervs. It was the best way I knew to try on, test out and confirm my femininity without actually having sex. (And that's having been raised by hippie parents who compared the spiritual magic of sex to "two star systems colliding in outer space.")

That sexual rite of passage remains, but today's teens have an entirely different notion of privacy than past generations. They grew up in the exhibitionistic Web culture of LiveJournal, YouTube and MySpace. They've seen girls on TV playfully jiggling their breasts for plastic beads, "Real World" cast members boldly screwing in front of cameras, Britney flashing her bald lady parts. These days, why would a girl be concerned about her silly topless snapshot circulating around school?

That's certainly the case with 16-year-old Melissa, a student at a high school near Greensburg-Salem, who has never worried about any of the X-rated pictures she's shared, because she cropped her face out of the photos, so "no one could identify me unless like [they] lifted up my shirt to figure it out haha," she wrote in a message sent on the blog platform Xanga. On her profile page, a rap song with the lyrics "I jus' wanna act like a porno flick actor" plays. It also exhibits a self-portrait she took with a cellphone camera of her reflection in a floor-length mirror; the sassy expression on her face matches the page's background: a sexy hot pink and lime green leopard print.

X-Rated Photos Make the Rounds

Joey, an 18-year-old who graduated from a San Francisco high school last year, has gotten X-rated snapshots from girls on his phone, through e-mail and on his MySpace page since he was 15. Some were longtime girlfriends that he swapped photos with and others were girls he'd just casually met; some pictures were suggestive, others were explicit. . . .

Typically, kiddie porn is seen as exponentially harmful because it's more than the original sexual abuse: It allows for a reliving of the trauma every time another pervert gets ahold of the material.

"Older adults have a short memory. There were things we did—people flashed each other and played spin the bottle," says Elizabeth Schroeder, director of Answer, Rutgers University's program dedicated to promoting sexuality education. "This is this generation's way of doing that." Heather Corinna, the 38-year old founder of Scarleteen, a Web site that provides sex-positive education for young adults, agrees: "Before we had this media, we had video cameras, before that film cameras, before that the written word, and all throughout, public or semi-public sex, ways of proclaiming to peers that one is sexually active or available to become so," she says.

But, clearly, there is a big difference between testifying on the wall of the boy's bathroom about the toe-curling blow jobs the school's head cheerleader gives and sending your buddies photographic proof. These digital offerings bring the potential for humiliation and blackmail if the photos or video get into the wrong hands—and, let's face it, they often do. Acting as your girlfriend's personal porno star is one thing; ending up a pedophile's favorite child pinup is quite another.

Protecting Without Victimizing Youth

There's good reason to be concerned about teens being self-pornographers. But many, especially legal experts, are disturbed by the fact that a healthy horn-dog of a teenager could be grouped in the same criminal category as a clinically ill pedophile. "These cases are picturing these teenagers as both predators and victims of themselves," says Amy Adler, a law professor at New York University who has studied child porn laws. "Child porn law was founded on a very different vision of what the major threat was."

That major threat, of course, is supposed to be adults who produce and peddle child smut. Reed Lee, a Chicago attorney and board member of the Free Speech Coalition, says: "A law to protect victims shouldn't send those very victims to jail."

Typically, kiddie porn is seen as exponentially harmful because it's more than the original sexual abuse: It allows for a reliving of the trauma every time another pervert gets ahold of the material. But "if the initial photograph was not taken as part of a traumatic episode and was, like it or not, part of a more normal teenage experience, the abuse rationale becomes hard to see," Adler argues. Still, plenty of child pornography cases have been prosecuted where the original photo is awfully benign—for example, a family picture taken at a nudist camp that is discovered by a pedophile and then cropped to reveal only the naked kid.

But it's tough to impress those kinds of nuances on kids, says Los Angeles criminal defense attorney Jeffrey Douglas. He once spoke to a high school class and tried to explain that, even though everyone seems to be "sexting," it "can literally destroy your life." The response? A boy rolled his eyes while making a grand jack-off gesture. "It's just the bullshit that adults tell them when they come to talk to them," he said. "It's tragically funny."

Sexting and Its Cultural Meaning

Douglas points out that the bungled law reveals fascinating cultural conflicts about childhood and teen sexuality. "I think the problem originates from the pathological fear that our culture, particularly the legal part of the culture, takes toward juvenile sexuality." He has defended numerous child porn cases and says prosecutors will treat the exchange of trial evidence like "an undercover heroin deal." Douglas says, "The fear is so enormous that it's like you're dealing with something radioactive. They don't consider the context or the meaning."

The context here is that teens are undertaking the sexploration that our porned culture at once dictates and forbids—in the same way that girls are taught that there is desirable validation in their sexuality and then are shamed for actually being sexual. Rutgers' Elizabeth Schroeder says an example of this contradiction is that sex educators like herself have to fight an uphill battle just to get into schools, while all it takes is a click of a button and a kid can catch an episode of "G-String Divas." She once asked a group of 12-year-old boys what they thought it meant to be a girl and the first response was: "Girls are here to give lap dances to boys."

12

Sexting Among Teenagers Is Not Child Pornography

Mike Galanos

Mike Galanos hosts Prime News, *a show that encourages debate, on HLN (formerly CNN Headline News).*

Sexting is a frightening new habit among teenagers, not least of all because boys are often pressuring girls to send nude pictures of themselves via their phone. Sexually charged pictures can have lasting, negative impacts on children's lives, and society should devise appropriate consequences for such behavior, including kicking them off sports teams or having them do community service. Branding teenagers as criminal offenders and pornographers does a disservice to them. Society needs to educate them, not criminalize their behavior.

"Sexting."

Have parents out there ever even heard of this term?

Whether you want to admit it or not, teenagers are sending sexual messages and naked pictures of themselves to their boyfriends and girlfriends. In most cases it's the girl sending a picture or message to the guy.

If you're thinking to yourself right now, "What's the big deal?" then you should think again. This practice can ruin our teenagers' lives.

Six teens in Greensburg, Pennsylvania, were charged as juveniles with possessing child pornography after three girls sent nude or semi-nude pictures of themselves to three boys.

Mike Galanos, "Is 'Sexting' Child Pornography?" CNN.com, April 8, 2009. Copyright © 2009 CNN.com. Courtesy CNN. Reprinted with permission.

It gets even worse.

Sexting Is a Serious Crime

A 13-year-old boy in Middletown, Ohio, is facing felony pandering obscenities charges after taping a sex act and showing it to friends at a skating party. A felony? Yes this kid needs to be punished but we don't need our 13- or 14-year-olds charged with child porn and lumped in with adult pedophiles and labeled as sex offenders.

It's clear we need to change our laws to catch up with technology.

I've spoken with several attorneys on our show [*Prime News*] and it seems there is no one reason prosecutors are opting to charge teens with child porn instead of lesser charges. Some may be doing it to "send a message."

Some may feel they have an obligation to charge these teens with the most serious offense possible and, according to the law, naked pictures of underage kids are usually considered child porn. And others may feel they are left with no options since there aren't really any laws that apply specifically to sexting.

In any case, it's clear we need to change our laws to catch up with technology.

A great illustration of why change is needed now is the story of Phillip Alpert, of Orlando, Florida. He didn't ask, but his girlfriend sexted him naked pictures of herself, according to the *Orlando Sentinel*. When they broke up, he mass e-mailed the photos to get back at her. Alpert, 18, was convicted of transmission of child porn and he will carry the label of "sex offender" until he is 43. He lost friends, was kicked out of school, he can't even move in with his dad because his dad lives near a school.

Punishment Might Be Too Harsh

Should Phillip be punished? Yes. Should the six teens in Pennsylvania face consequences? Yes. But let's kick them off cheerleading squads and sports teams. Make them do community service and take classes on sex crimes. Educate other teens on the dangers of sexting. Pay a price, yes, but these young people shouldn't pay for this for the rest of their lives.

And if you think this couldn't happen to your kid, think again. Sexting is more prevalent than you think.

The National Campaign to Prevent Teen and Unplanned Pregnancy teamed up with CosmoGirl.com and asked over 1,200 teens about their sexual behaviors in cyberspace.

According to their study, 39 percent of teens (that's ages 13–19) are sending or posting sexually suggestive messages over IM, text or e-mail and around the same number of teens are receiving such messages. Half of those teens, 20 percent, are sending or posting nude or semi-nude pictures of themselves. That's frightening.

Why are our kids doing this?

On our show, psychotherapist Stacy Kaiser said, "What I'm finding is a lot of girls are doing this because they're hoping it will help them get or keep a boyfriend." The numbers agree with Stacy.

According to the study, 51 percent of girls say it's "pressure from guys" that's making them send sexual messages and pictures of themselves. So guys are expecting this and our girls are saying "OK." It makes me wonder how much progress we've really made in how young women are viewed and treated.

The bottom line: We need to educate, not incarcerate, our teens and it has to start with parents.

Don't let the culture indoctrinate your little boy or girl about sex before their time. So strike first as a parent. If your kids are older, let them know a digital record is for life. When little Suzie tries to win the affection of little Bobby by sexting him a picture, she is putting her future at stake. There is no control over that image or video once it gets out. But that doesn't mean little Suzie should be charged as a child pornographer.

13

Sexting Marks a Cultural and Generational Shift

Peggy O'Crowley

Peggy O'Crowley is a frequent contributor to NJ.com and other online publications.

The problem with sexting is not that teenagers do not understand that sending nude pictures can be harmful and land them in front of a judge, but that teenagers do not care much about the consequences. They grow up with technologies at their disposal that their parents did not have and in many cases do not use or only marginally comprehend. The best way to deal with teenagers' recklessness is to punish them by confiscating cell phones and other gadgets, rather than treating them as pornographers. A major cultural shift separates them from their parents' generation, not an increase in criminal behavior.

Jane, a North Jersey teen,[1] knows posting nude pictures on Facebook is inappropriate. She knows she can get into deep trouble and cause embarrassment for herself and her family.

The problem is kids like Jane don't care.

Their behavior is called "sexting"—sending sexually suggestive messages or images to others via cell phone, or posting them on social websites such as Facebook and MySpace. And

1. Jane is a real North Jersey teen, but *Inside Jersey* is not using her actual name to protect her privacy.

Peggy O'Crowley, "The Sexting Generation," *Inside Jersey*, August 13, 2009. Copyright © 2009 Inside Jersey-nj.com. Reprinted with permission.

as a new school calendar begins, parents and officials are hoping to get teens to understand the kind of serious trouble they can get into by sexting.

At the least they're hoping kids don't pick up where they left off at summer break.

Last spring [2009], two 14-year-old girls in separate cases, in Glen Rock and Clifton, were caught transmitting nude pictures—something that technically is a violation of child pornography laws under the Adam Walsh Child Protection and Safety Act, passed in 2006.

In the Glen Rock case, however, police told students who had received a nude picture of the female student on their cell phones to delete it. The district then held assemblies on cyber awareness for middle and high school students.

The Clifton girl caught sexting was ordered to complete six months of counseling.

Surveys show that between 20 and 40 percent of teenagers admit they have sexted.

Might Face Severe Punishment

In other parts of the country, however, teens caught sexting have been charged with possession and distribution of child pornography. Some are facing years on sex offender registries, which make it impossible to continue attending school or even get a job.

In a Pennsylvania sexting incident involving pictures of two girls in their underwear, the American Civil Liberties Union [ACLU] intervened, arguing the images were not child pornography but an expression of freedom of speech under the First Amendment.

"We think this is more appropriately addressed within the family structure," says Edward Barocas, legal director of the ACLU of New Jersey.

Surveys show that between 20 and 40 percent of teenagers admit they have sexted.

Cynthia Lam, 15, of Westfield, thinks teens are more likely to text sexy messages than send erotic pictures. "What's more common is seductive text messaging as a flirty thing. They can be very promiscuous while texting, but not nude pictures," says Lam, who writes for *Sex, Etc.*, an educational newsletter by teens and for teens published by Answer, a national sexuality education organization for adolescents based at Rutgers University in New Brunswick.

"But putting up pictures of yourself (on a social networking site) in a bikini or exposed clothing is pretty common. You want to look good; it's your profile," she says. Elizabeth Schroeder, executive director of Answer, says it's not the behavior, but the technology that's new.

"Technology is much more far-reaching and permanent, and teenagers are not consequential thinkers. . . . They are pushing boundaries around sexuality. Years ago they would flash someone or moon someone or write notes or start rumors," says Schroeder, who has a doctorate in human sexuality education.

Now, they can use cell phones and computers to act out sexually.

Teens also use revenge sexting, or malicious sexting—in which someone sends compromising pictures of another—as a form of humiliation.

Displaying Confidence

"I guess it's our new way of trying to get attention. It's a measure of your confidence. And the easiest way to display it is how confident you feel in your body," says Anita Modi, 17, of South Brunswick.

Modi also believes the preponderance of sexy images of young actresses and models fuels teens to exhibit their sexuality more openly.

"I see a lot of young girls, tweens, teens, college age," says Susan Lipkins, a New York psychologist who works with children and adolescents. "About four to five years ago I saw a shift in the way they think about their bodies and sexuality."

Today, boys and girls alike are interested in no-strings-attached sex because, she says, "they think having a relationship is too much work."

"One 13-year-old girl told me, 'I've always been told I am equal, and I am equal to have sex, too.' For young people, sexting is part of their everyday communication system—it's a mating call, a form of gossip," she says.

Teens also use revenge sexting, or malicious sexting—in which someone sends compromising pictures of another—as a form of humiliation.

Ruth, who asked to be identified only by her middle name because she is a high school teacher in Essex County, says she has seen male students distribute inappropriate pictures of female students as revenge after the break up of a relationship.

Last year [2008] a student at her school was suspended for revenge sexting, she says.

A Fairly Common Practice

According to a non-weighted survey Lipkins conducted, 66 percent of 323 people questioned between ages 13 and 72 say they had engaged in sexting. She presented her findings last May [2009] at a conference on the internet and mental health held at McGill University.

The most cited survey on sexting, however, was commissioned by CosmoGirl.com and the National Campaign to Prevent Teen and Unplanned Pregnancy. Twenty percent of teenagers, and one third of young adults 20 to 26, say they had electronically sent or posted online nude or seminude pictures of themselves.

Also, nearly 40 percent of teens and 60 percent of young adults said they had sent sexually suggestive messages via text, e-mail or instant message. "Is it upsetting? To a lot of us older folk, this is fundamentally a question of public behavior versus private behavior, which seems to be at least a moving target for young people. The notion that you'd share nude pictures over the Internet just doesn't compute for an older person," says Bill Alpert, a spokesman for the campaign.

While parents should be aware of what their kids are doing with their cell phones and computers, the findings aren't cause for panic, he says. After all, about 80 percent of teens say they were not transmitting nude pictures, he says.

Maria Concilio, of South Orange, a mother of three—including two girls ages 12 and 14—says she has heard of sexting, but is certain "my kids won't do it."

Parents Need to Supervise Teens

Why? Because Concilio says she is vigilant about checking her daughters' cell phone texts and Facebook accounts. The same with Katie McGrath, of West Orange, a mother of three sons who are 15, 22, and 24. "I'm always on his phone," she says of her youngest. And she'll continue to monitor it "if he wants me to keep on paying for it."

The CosmoGirl.com survey also found that slightly more girls than boys said they sexted. And while most said it was a "fun and flirtatious activity," about half of the girls said they were pressured by a guy to send sexually suggestive content.

Only 18 percent of the boys say their girlfriends pushed them into it.

"We need to talk to boys to never pressure anyone into it, and girls shouldn't feel pressured," says Schroeder. "That said, it's true that many girls will do anything to get and keep a boyfriend."

Lipkins rejects that argument, however. Her survey found that only two percent of girls said they felt pressured to sext.

The concern over girls may well be a societal double standard about female sexuality, says Peter Cumming, a professor of children's studies at York University in Toronto who has written about sexting.

"I think the hysteria has it backwards. I've seen articles that say technology fuels youth sexuality. I like to think that would happen to two people left on an island together if we forgot to give them cell phones."

John Shehan, director of the Exploited Child Division of the National Center for Missing and Exploited Children, doesn't share the opinion that sexting is harmless. He believes it's risky behavior that can have serious consequences beyond getting in trouble at school. A teen's erotic image can end up on the screens of pornographers.

"These people collect these images like your average citizen collects baseball cards. They save them and redistribute them," says Shehan. "The content can live out there forever."

A cell phone is a privilege, not a right. So the consequence should be immediate and should be tied to the technology.

Peer Pressure Is a Serious Concern

Sometimes teen boys will try to collect images of girls in their school, he says. "It's a power play; the boys will threaten to use the image if they don't get more for their collage."

Shehan says communication, not monitoring keystrokes, is the way parents should deal with their kids. . . . Ideally, parents should be talking to their children about issues of sexuality, privacy and appropriate boundaries long before they come across seminude pictures on their kids' social networking pages, says Schroeder.

And there should be consequences for bad behavior, she says. "A cell phone is a privilege, not a right. So the consequence should be immediate and should be tied to the technology." She advises parents to take the cell phone away for awhile. But Lipkins believes there is little adults can do, and young people know it. Her sexting survey seems to support that opinion.

About half say they posted suggestive or erotic images even though they already realized the material could get them in trouble in school or at work. Most also say they were aware it could cause personal and family embarrassment. Says Schroeder: "They think we're dinosaurs and we don't get it, and they're right. This is a cultural shift, a piece of a puzzle in a larger picture."

14

Sexting Teens Should Be Taught Self-Respect

Warren Binford

Warren Binford directs the Clinical Law Program at Willamette University College of Law. She has worked as a child advocate and has served as a Court-Appointed Special Advocate (CASA) for abused and neglected children in the United States. She has also worked with the International Red Cross on numerous issues relating to child soldiers and other child victims of war.

Sexting, while not a desirable activity for minors, is born of an awakening sense of sexuality and self-expression, and is not aimed primarily at hurting others. Children have not yet acquired an adult's sense of propriety, and they cannot be expected to foresee the consequences of their actions. Parents and schools need to educate them about their behavior, but teenagers should not be thrown in jail for the sake of laws that seek to protect them.

There is an old saying that "children are great imitators, so give them something great to imitate." Unfortunately, we seem to be failing the next generation in this regard.

Take "sexting," for example. News stories have been popping up around the country about teenagers sending nude or semi-nude pictures of themselves and others to friends via text messages on their cell phones. Our response? We threaten to "jail 'em" using child pornography laws.

Warren Binford, "'Sexting' Solutions: Teach Teens Self-Respect," OregonLive.com, April 4, 2009. Copyright © 2009 by Oregon Live. Reproduced by permission of the author.

The idea of prosecuting children for violating laws that were intended to protect them is more than ironic; it's hypocritical.

Society Uses Sex to Sell and Provoke

Anyone who goes online using an unfiltered computer is bombarded by images of nude and seminude bodies. We receive pop-up ads that use the body to promote goods and services. We receive pictures of penises in spam e-mails peddling male virility drugs. Skype messages appear on our computer screens from total strangers, inviting us to look at "nude pics of me," and Internet news pages splash image after image of celebrities wearing sexy clothes in provocative poses.

Just last week [March 2009] a former elementary school classmate of mine bombarded me and all her other Facebook friends with a series of pictures of herself in sexually enticing poses, wearing nothing more than a minuscule bikini and declaring, "Yes. It really is me!" Apparently, even middle-age professors get sexted.

First and foremost, we must never forget that they are still children.

How did we get to a place in our society where grown women feel compelled to bare their bodies to childhood friends on Facebook? And is it any wonder that our teenagers are doing the same?

From early childhood, our children are bombarded with sexual images. They quickly come to believe that this is how we communicate to each other—body image to body image. With teenagers' mastery of modern technology, we are quickly learning, they can convey their body images even faster and distribute them more widely than most adults can. No wonder we're scared.

Living in a "Gone Wild" World

So how, as a society, do we respond to this national epidemic of teenagers "gone wild"?

First, we look to ourselves to ensure that we, both individually and as a society, are giving the next generation "something great to imitate."

Second, we try to expose children only to age-appropriate media that are consistent with the values we want them to emulate.

Third, we make sure that we have close, communicative relationships with our children in which we teach them about the power and beauty of the human body. We help them learn to care for and respect their bodies—not advertise, use and then trash them like just another throwaway commodity in a consumer-driven culture.

What do we do with the kids who cross the line of decency and respect for their bodies or the bodies of others?

Teens Are Not Adults

First and foremost, we must never forget that they are still children. Scientific research in the past 10 years shows us what parents have known for millennia: Teenagers are not fully functioning adults. We should not expect them to be. Their brains are still rapidly developing.

During adolescence, children undergo tremendous neurological growth and have significant problems controlling their impulses, understanding the long-term consequences of their actions and using reasoning. These are developmentally normal behaviors for adolescents.

Does it make their behavior OK? Of course not. We must expect great things from our children if we want them to fulfill their potential. But when they disappoint us, we shouldn't simply throw them in jail and deprive them of healthy neurological stimuli when they need it most. Instead, we must face the fact that our teenagers are still children, despite what their changing bodies suggest, and design a corrective program that will help rather than hurt them.

15

The Sexting Panic Is Threatening Educators

Virginia Education Association

With over sixty thousand educator members across the state, the Virginia Education Association is the state of Virginia's largest education organization and an advocate for quality public education.

After investigating a sexting case in his Virginia high school, Ting-Yi Oei, an assistant principal, was charged with possession of child pornography, simply because he saved the picture in question so that law enforcement would be able to use it as evidence. While the case against him was very weak, the panic surrounding sexting made it nearly impossible for the educator to save his reputation as reports of his arrest spread via the Internet. The charges were finally dropped, but the case reveals how vulnerable educators can be to the hysteria generated by overzealous prosecutors, parents, and online media.

Ting-Yi Oei, a Loudoun Education Association (LEA) member and assistant principal, is back to work this fall supervising students at Freedom High School in South Riding. But the horror show he endured this past year [2008] before baseless charges were thrown out by a judge in March [2009] illustrates the perils faced by every educator as new technologies fast outpace school policies and procedures. . . .

A former Fulbright exchange teacher and a Quaker, Oei had never heard of "sexting," the sending of racy pictures

Virginia Education Association, "Techno-Trap," VEANEA.com, 2009. Copyright © 2009 by Virginia Education Association (VEA). Reproduced by permission.

from one cell phone to another, when he headed to his office at Freedom High on March 14, 2008. But on that day a teacher told him she'd heard a rumor that students may have been sending or receiving such images. Oei questioned a 17-year-old student in the presence of the school safety and security specialist, and the boy admitted he did have such a picture on his phone. When Oei looked at the image, he saw the torso of a female in her underwear with arms crossed over her breasts; her head was not visible. The boy said he did not know who the female was or who had sent him the picture.

Local television news appeared to play it straight, but just the mug shot and mere fact of the accusation were enough to sully Oei's reputation.

Oei took the picture to Freedom High's principal, who instructed him to save the image on his computer in case it was needed later. But how to transfer the image from the cell phone to a computer? Oei was stumped and called the school technology specialist into the room. Maybe some kind of cable? No, but it's easy, the boy said. I'll forward the message to your cell phone; then you can send it from your cell phone to your e-mail address and save it on your computer. So Oei, who'd never received or sent a text message or picture on his cell phone in his life—and with the best of intentions—pressed the button that could have undone everything he'd worked for in his 35-year career.

Case Not Closed

Subsequent investigation by Oei and other school officials did not yield the identity of the female in the photo. So after reporting his findings to the school principal, Oei thought the matter was closed. But it was only beginning.

Two weeks later, the same boy was caught "flagging" a female student (pulling her pants down) in class, and Oei suspended him. During a conversation with the boy's mother, Oei mentioned the earlier sexting incident. That lit the fuse. The mother, Oei says, blasted him for not reporting the earlier incident to her and demanded the flagging suspension be revoked or she'd see him "in court."

Shortly thereafter, investigators from the sheriff's office came to the school in response, they said, to a parent's complaint about inappropriate photos being sent by cell phone. Oei told them what he knew about the March incident and was asked if he had the picture. Oei couldn't find the picture on his computer and remembered it was on his cell phone. Not able to locate the photo himself, he offered the cell phone to investigators, who located the image and forwarded it to their own phone. They thanked Oei, returned his phone, and left. At that moment, the soft-spoken administrator thought he'd done everything by the book. But he was about to become the fall guy. And when he learned the following month that he was being charged with a misdemeanor count of "failure to report" child abuse, one of his first calls was to the LEA, which connected him with a local attorney, Jim Faughnan.

Possession of Child Pornography

The failure-to-report charge, Oei and Faughnan maintained, couldn't be sustained because Oei did not know if the person in the photo was a minor and, in any case, he had followed the law's mandate to report the incident to superiors. But he was placed on administrative leave . . . and hoped for the best. And the failure-to-report charge *was* dismissed—but to Oei's shock an even more serious felony charge of possessing child pornography was filed in its place.

So on August 20, 2008, notwithstanding his offer to turn himself in if indicted, Oei was pulled out of a school meeting, handcuffed, and taken to jail. County prosecutor Jim Plowman later added two misdemeanor charges of contributing to the delinquency of a minor against Oei for possessing the single image on both his cell phone and computer.

At that point, "my world turned topsy-turvy," Oei recalls. He was assigned to work in a school division testing office with no contact with students. His legal bills mounted (eventually topping $167,000), and he took out a second mortgage on his home. He lost weight and had trouble sleeping. Above all, as the legal process dragged on in late 2008 and early 2009, Oei agonized with the stigma of being accused of a sex crime. Local television news appeared to play it straight, but just the mug shot and mere fact of the accusation were enough to sully Oei's reputation.

The Internet was a free-for-all. Oei was dragged through the mud on blogs like BadBadTeacher.com. In a particularly loathsome example, his mug shot and a lifted newspaper story were posted on a blog called "Faces of Child Porn" based solely on the fact of his arrest.

Oei's case also raises questions about how educators can stay ahead of the tech-curve as new mobile devices, video, and photo applications are created every day.

The Charges Are Dropped

It wasn't until March 2009 that someone other than Oei's defense took a clear-headed look at the facts of the case and the law. That was Circuit Court Judge Thomas Horne, and he dismissed all charges, noting that the cell phone image did not come close to meeting the definition of pornography. Oei was jubilant, and in a meeting of LEA supporters a month later, he emphasized that "this case should never have gotten that far."

To Oei's defenders, his case is an object lesson in how educators are vulnerable to over-reaching prosecutors. Plowman wanted to appear tough on sex crime, and the media reported that he was also unhappy with the way the Loudoun school system had dealt with some previous incidents. Several times, prosecutors told Oei that if he resigned, the charges would go away. He stood his ground. "My wife and I decided we wouldn't succumb to that, because education is just too important a part of my life. Everything I'd done for 30 years was on the line," Oei said.

So how did the prosecution go so wrong?

Attorney Steve Stone, who represented Oei in the criminal case, thinks the answer is fairly simple. Plowman, Stone told the *Loudoun Independent* recently, never had the facts to bring a case in the first place. "He didn't do his homework," Stone says of Plowman. "He never read the cases. How could you not know the state of the law and still bring the charges?"

And it wasn't just Oei and his supporters accusing Plowman of improperly filing the case. In an editorial, the *Washington Post* excoriated Plowman, questioning "why criminal charges were ever brought against an unassuming assistant principal who was just trying to do his job." And it went on to ask, "Will teachers and administrators hesitate in the future to exercise their rightful authority for fear of vengeful parents and zealous prosecutors?"

Educators Lag Behind

Oei's case also raises questions about how educators can stay ahead of the tech-curve as new mobile devices, video, and photo applications are created every day. Most schools are still trying to get a handle on cell phone cheating and Web plagiarism, and the outbreak of sexting caught them off-guard. Oei says his case has prompted discussions of how best to handle incidents of sexting that educators may come across ("When in doubt, report it to law enforcement"), but who knows what will happen when the next device finds its way into students' hands?

In the past year, teens in several states have been charged under child pornography laws for either sending or receiving and forwarding "sexts." A conviction can mean not only jail time or probation but placement on an official list of sex offenders. But Oei is one of many who question whether a teen guilty of a lapse in judgment ought to be treated the same way as a child predator.

"There has got to be something less severe than teenagers texting each other with this sort of thing being considered child pornographers," says Oei. "Being placed in a sex offender registry is something that would harm them the rest of their lives."

16

Sexting Is a Modern Dating Instrument for Adults

Jessica Leshnoff

Jessica Leshnoff is a journalist and copywriter, publishing articles in lifestyle magazines and national newspapers. She contributes to Baltimore Magazine *and* AARP.org.

Despite popular belief, sexting is used not only by teenagers. More and more people over fifty are using provocative messages and nude pictures as dating devices. Yet while many agree that it helps to spice up their sex lives, others are disappointed by people who send old and misleading pictures. And for some, having a sexually explicit photo sent to a cell phone is uncomfortable and embarrassing.

When Roger gets to an intimate stage with a woman these days, it usually doesn't take long until the sexy photos start. His dating partners either request that he send them a suggestive—or downright explicit—photo from his cell phone to theirs, or they just send one themselves, completely unsolicited.

"I'll say, 'You have an amazing body. You have amazing breasts,'" he reports. "The next thing you know, you'll get a picture of a breast," he says with a hearty laugh.

Sexting as a Dating Tool

The Massachusetts resident has been enjoying the high-tech flirtation for years now, taking part in a trend the mainstream media has dubbed "sexting," a play on the term "texting"

Jessica Leshnoff, "C*U*2nite: Sexting Not Just for Kids," AARP.org, November 2009. Copyright © 2009 by American Association of Retired Persons (AARP). Reproduced by permission of the author.

("sex" plus "text" equals "sext"). The term has made headlines recently, as teens continually get themselves in sticky situations with a form of high-speed communication that thrives on informality, spontaneity, and—for many young folks—bad judgment.

More and more of the 50+ set, both single and married, are using text messaging to spice up their sex lives.

The catch is, Roger isn't a teenager—or even a 20-something. He's a 59-year-old divorcé, and, thanks to his cell phone and a slew of sassy ladies, his love life is more interesting than ever.

Shocked? Don't be. More and more of the 50+ set, both single and married, are using text messaging to spice up their sex lives. Boomers, often sandwiched between teenagers, aging parents, and busy work schedules, are taking advantage of the new technology because it's fast, easy, and fun.

Relationship coach Suzanne Blake has seen and heard it all when it comes to sexting, including a wife who enjoys sexting her husband while he's traveling on business, telling (and showing) him what he's missing at home. While this may surprise some, Blake's not surprised at all.

"It's a misnomer that the biological changes of aging have to lead to a decrease in sexuality and sexual experience," she says.

Feeling Young and Sexual

Whether they're single and casually dating, married, or in long-term relationships, "Boomers want sexual activity," Blake explains. "They want to flirt. It makes them feel lively and young."

Jill, 50, certainly feels fresh and vital when she sexts.

"It makes you a little more brave," she says. "It takes the fear away, your inhibitions. I might be a little more bold in a text message than I would be over the phone or in person."

Sexting also makes the South Carolina nurse, who's been divorced for 15 years and enjoys casual dating, feel as if she had a "naughty secret."

"If you're sitting in a restaurant waiting for your food, you can just talk dirty to someone, and no one knows what you're doing," Jill says, in a slow Southern drawl. "I would rather talk on the phone. But I'm also comfortable with hiding behind texting if I want to say something dirty."

That's exactly the appeal of sexting, according to New York City psychotherapist and advice columnist Dr. Jonathan Alpert.

Because there's no anticipation of a direct verbal response, there's less at stake than if the conversation were being held the old-fashioned method: face-to-face, he says. "Where there's less risk of being critiqued or judged, there's opportunity for greater sexual expression."

It also fits nicely into longtime couples' busy schedules to keep things spicy, says relationship and sexual health expert Genie James, who recommends sexting to couples who need to travel away from one another or have trouble connecting throughout the day.

"It's cheap," she says. "It's quick. It's right there. And nobody can hear you."

Not everyone likes receiving a sexually charged text or photo pop up on her phone as much as she thought she would.

Keeping a Relationship Interesting

James continues, "It's about setting the stage for sex and keeping passion alive. A cell phone's in your hands every day. You're already doing it."

But beware, the experts warn. Sexting has its dangers, too, especially when it comes to people in the dating world.

One of the biggies? False advertising, says relationship expert Dr. Gilda Carle. It's something online daters may be all too familiar with when their date shows up looking about 30 years older than his profile photo.

"They're overselling and over-promising," she says of big-talking sexters. "I think too much, too soon in relationships is not such a great thing. I suggest to people that you grow the relationship outside the bedroom so that when you come into the bedroom, it's your playpen."

Then there's the comfort factor. Not everyone likes receiving a sexually charged text or photo pop up on her phone as much as she thought she would.

Richard, 66, received an X-rated photo on his cell phone from a potential online date recently and surprised himself by being less than thrilled.

"It was a little bit embarrassing," the Iowa resident says sheepishly. "Well, it was very embarrassing."

The fact that he was with a group of colleagues after hours at a restaurant didn't help matters, either.

Sexting might be an interesting experiment, he says with a sigh, but after his experience, "It was like the fun kind of went out of it."

Organizations to Contact

The editors have compiled the following list of organizations concerned with the issues debated in this book. The descriptions are derived from materials provided by the organizations. All have publications or information available for interested readers. The list was compiled on the date of publication of the present volume; the information provided here may change. Readers need to remember that many organizations take several weeks or longer to respond to inquiries.

Beatbullying
+44 20 8771-3377 • fax: +44 20 8771-8550
e-mail: info@beatbullying.org
website: www.beatbullying.org

Beatbullying works with children and teenagers across the United Kingdom to provide important opportunities to change their lives and outlook positively. In particular, the organization works with those so deeply affected by bullying that they fear going to school. Beatbullying also seeks to effect change in bullies' behavior, working with them to take responsibility and a sense of ownership over their actions. Videos, news, and "lesson plans," like the "Friendship and Peer Pressure Lesson Plan" are available online.

Childnet International
Studio 14 Brockley Cross Business Centre, 96 Endwell Rd.
London SE4 2PD
+44 20 7639-6967 • fax: +44 20 7639-7027
e-mail info@childnet.com
website: www.childnet.com

Childnet International is dedicated to helping young people use the Internet constructively. The organization gives Internet safety advice and links for children, teenagers, parents, and teachers. Policy papers and annual reviews are available online.

ConnectSafely
www.connectsafely.org

ConnectSafely is a forum for parents, teens, educators, and advocates designed to give teens and parents a voice in the public discussion about youth online safety. The site offers tips for safe social networking as well as other resources.

Cyberbully411
website: www.cyberbully411.org

Cyberbully411 provides resources and opportunities for discussion and sharing for teenagers who want to know more about—or have been victims of—online harassment. The website was created by the nonprofit Internet Solutions for Kids, Inc. and invites teenagers to share their stories or download tips and information on cyberbullying, depression, and other relevant topics.

Federal Trade Commission (FTC)
600 Pennsylvania Ave. NW, Washington, DC   20580
(202) 326-2222
website: www.ftc.gov

The FTC deals with issues of everyday economic life. It is the only federal agency with both consumer protection and competition jurisdiction. The FTC strives to enforce laws and regulations and to advance consumers' interests by sharing its expertise with federal and state legislatures and US and international government agencies. Publications such as "Social Networking Sites: A Parent's Guide" can be downloaded from its website.

Institute for Responsible Online and Cell-Phone Communication (I.R.O.C.²)
PO Box 1131, 200 Walt Whitman Ave.
Mount Laurel, NJ   08054-9998
(877) 295-2005
website: www.iroc2.org

I.R.O.C.[2] is a nonprofit organization advocating digital responsibility, safety, and awareness. It endorses the development and safe use of all digital devices (e.g., digital cameras, cell phones, computers, Internet, video cameras, web cameras, etc.) and the World Wide Web. The organization's creation is based on the fact that many individuals are not aware of the short- and long-term consequences of their own actions when utilizing digital technologies. Articles on social networking and sexting are available at the website.

International Association for the Wireless Telecommunications Industry (CTIA)

1400 Sixteenth St. NW, Ste. 600, Washington, DC   20036
(202) 736-3200 • fax: (202) 785-0721
e-mail: RRoche@ctia.org
website: www.ctia.org

CTIA is an international nonprofit membership organization founded in 1984, representing all sectors of wireless communications—cellular, personal communication services, and enhanced specialized mobile radio. Information on wireless safety is available on its website.

Internet Keep Safe Coalition

1401 K St. NW, Ste. 600, Washington, DC   20005
(202) 587-5583 • fax: (202) 737-4097
e-mail: info@ikeepsafe.org
website: www.iKeepSafe.org

iKeepSafe.org—which features Faux Paw the Techno Cat—is a coalition of forty-nine governors and their spouses, law enforcement, the American Medical Association, the American Academy of Pediatrics, and other associations dedicated to helping parents, educators, and caregivers by providing information and guidelines to teach children the safe use of technology.

Internet Solutions for Kids, Inc.

1820 E. Garry Ave., Ste. 105, Santa Ana, CA   92705

(949) 705-6992 • toll-free fax: (877) 362-1629
e-mail: info@isolutions4kids.org
website: http://is4k.com

Internet Solutions for Kids, a nonprofit research organization explores the impact of new technologies on adolescent health. The organziation seeks to promote innovative methods that improve the health and safety of young people, engaging in research as well as active youth education and support. The organization created the website Cyberbully411.org.

OnGuard Online

website: www.onguardonline.gov

OnGuardOnline provides practical tips from the federal government and the technology industry to help people be on guard against Internet fraud, secure their computer, and protect personal information. OnGuardOnline publishes tips for high school and college students on how to use social networking sites safely. Videos and games, such as "The Case of the Cyber Criminal," are available online.

Wired Safety

website: www.wiredsafety.org

WiredSafety is an Internet safety and help group. It provides educational material, news, assistance, and awareness on all aspects of cybercrime and abuse, privacy, security, and responsible technology use. It is also the parent group of Teen angels.org, FBI-trained teens and preteens who promote Internet safety.

Bibliography

Books

Julia Angwin	*Stealing MySpace: The Battle to Control the Most Popular Website in America*. New York: Random House, 2009.
Dave Awl	*Facebook Me! A Guide to Having Fun with Your Friends and Promoting Your Projects on Facebook*. Berkeley, CA: Peachpit Press, 2009.
Jack Balkin et al., eds.	*Cybercrime: Digital Cops in a Networked Environment*. New York: New York University Press, 2006.
David Crystal	*Txtng: The Gr8 Db8*. New York: Oxford University Press, 2008.
Charles Ess	*Digital Media Ethics: Digital Media and Society*. Cambridge: Polity Press, 2009.
Christina Garsten and Helena Wulff	*New Technologies at Work: People, Screens, and Social Virtuality*. Oxford: Berg, 2003.
Anastasia Goodstein	*Totally Wired: What Teens and Tweens Are Really Doing Online*. New York: St. Martin's Griffin, 2007.
Dennis Howitt and Kerry Sheldon	*Sex Offenders and the Internet*. New York: John Wiley, 2007.

Larry Magid and Elaine Collier	*MySpace Unraveled: A Parent's Guide to Teen Social Networking.* Berkeley, CA: Peachpit Press, 2007.
Samuel McQuade III, James Colt, and Nancy Meyer	*Cyber Bullying: Protecting Kids and Adults from Online Bullies.* Westport, CT: Praeger, 2009.
Mike Ribble and Gerald Bailey	*Digital Citizenship in Schools.* Eugene, OR: International Society for Technology in Education, 2007.
Laura Saba	*Textual Intercourse: Dating and Relating in a Cellular World.* Philadelphia: Running Press, 2009.
Mike Sullivan	*Online Predators.* Longwood, FL: Xulon Books, 2008.
Emily Vander Veer	*Facebook: The Missing Manual.* Cambridge, MA: Pogue Press, 2008.

Periodicals

Courtney Blanchard	"Sexting Flashes Across Nation, Tri-States," *Dubuque (IA)Telegraph-Herald*, April 21, 2009.
Bruce Bower	"Growing Up Online: Young People Jump Headfirst into the Internet's World," *Science News*, June 17, 2006.
Bruce Bower	"Internet Seduction: Online Sex Offenders Prey on At-Risk Teens," *Science News*, February 23, 2008.

Center for the Digital Future	"Annual Internet Survey by the Center for the Digital Future Finds Shifting Trends Among Adults About the Benefits and Consequences of Children Going Online," USC Annenberg School of Communications, 2008.
Christian Science Monitor	"'Sexting' Overreach," April 28, 2009.
Curriculum Review	"Teens Share Sexually Explicit Messages: Simple Rebellion or Dangerous Behavior?" May 2009.
Maryjoy Duncan	"The Serious Implications of 'Sexting,'" *El Chicano Weekly*, April 22, 2010.
Economist	"Primates on Facebook," February 26, 2009.
Leah Fabel	"Tips on How to Address Sexting," *Washington (DC) Examiner*, April 18, 2010.
Florida Parishes Bureau	"Loranger Teen Booked in Threats to Harm Other Teen, Cyberstalking," *Capital City Press*, July 12, 2007.
Lev Grossman	"The Hyperconnected," *Time*, April 5, 2007.
Ann Doss Helms	"Teachers Disciplined for Facebook Postings," *Charlotte (NC) Observer*, November 12, 2008.
Joshua Herman	"Sexting: It's No Joke, It's a Crime," *Illinois Bar Journal*, April 1, 2010.

Idaho State Journal	"Should Sexting Be a Crime?" April 4, 2010.
Monica Jones	"Your Child and the Internet: Tips to Keep Them Safe on the Information Superhighway," *Ebony*, March 2006.
Jeanine Kendle	"Sexting Can Leave a Mark for a Lifetime," *Wooster (OH) Daily Record*, May 5, 2010.
Lancaster (PA) New Era	"Flirting with 'Sexting' Remedy," April 4, 2009.
Jason Long	"Tips for School Administrators on How to Handle 'Sexting,'" *Mondaq Business Briefing*, April 13, 2010.
Maureen Macfarlane	"Misbehavior in Cyberspace: The Rise in Social Networking Sites and Chat Rooms Intermingles Free Expression and Student Safety in Cyberspace," *School Administrator*, October 2007.
Emily McFarlan	"Debating Legality of 'Sexting,'" *Elgin (IL) Courier News*, July 19, 2009.
Benjamin Radford	"Predator Panic: A Closer Look," *Skeptical Inquirer*, September 2006.
Paul Rodriguez	"Virtual Child Porn's Very Real Consequences," *Insight on the News*, May 27, 2002.
Christine Rosen	"Virtual Friendship and the New Narcissism," *New Atlantis*, 2007.

Brian Solis   "Cultural Voyeurism and Social Media," *Social Media Today*, March 17, 2008.

Bob Stiles   "Effort Begins to Standardize Sexting Penalty," *Pittsburgh Tribune-Review*, April 1, 2009.

Canan Tasci   "'Sexting' Among Teens Can Lead to Problems," *San Bernardino (CA) Sun*, December 6, 2009.

Clive Thomson "Brave New World of Digital Intimacy," *New York Times*, September 5, 2008.

U.S. Newswire "What Is Sexting? Why Is It a Problem? What Parents and Teens Need to Know," September 21, 2009.

Index